TO: ______________________________

Qualities Men Want & How to Get Them

Published 2023 by Frank Paul Vignola

Book cover and chapter covers designed by Frank Paul Vignola

Printed in the United States of America

First paperback edition

Library of Congress CIP Data
Names: Vignola, Frank P., author
Title: Crafting masculinity: qualities men want and how to
get them / Frank Paul Vignola
ISBN: 979-8-218-06382-5
Subjects: Self-help techniques. Social sciences. Life coach.
Masculinity. Psychology. Men's studies.

"No man is more unhappy than he who never faces adversity. For he is not permitted to prove himself."

– Seneca

THE CONTENTS

CRAFTING

MASCULINITY

Ch 1: The Dormant Beast

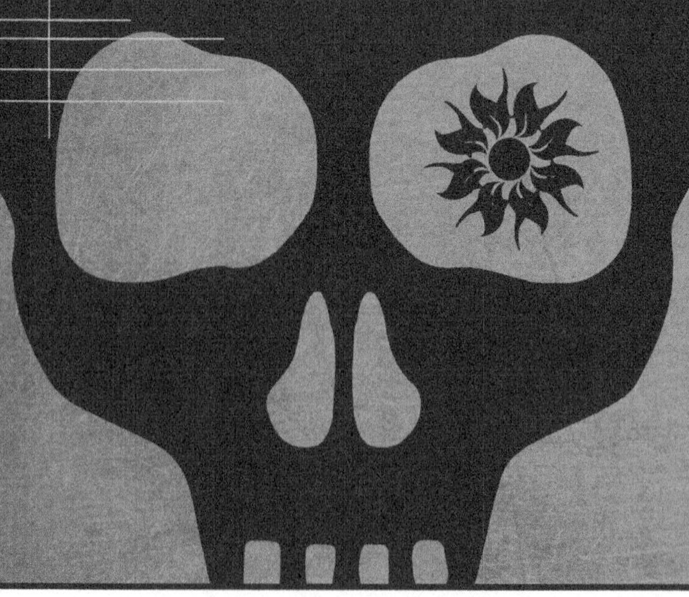

The man you are...............................the man you want to be.

And that **fucking gap**. I've spent the last decade coaching men and studying human behavior through a variety of interactive modalities and performing arts training trying to help men fill that gap. Coaching and the arts, two very different avenues to understanding the many sides of men, have given me the ability to peer into some of the deepest realms of that abyss. I've worked with men in their teens, men in their sixties, straight men, gay men, non-binary men, men of all different ethnicities and men from all parts of the world. I've seen the parallels in what these different men want, what motivates them most and the qualities they admire in other men and want for themselves. Every day I learn something new and every day I become more invested in trying to develop solutions to something a lot of men struggle with but don't talk about:

Masculinity.

I struggled a great deal with my own masculinity growing up. I felt inadequate as a boy. Overcoming that inadequacy and becoming a man I'm proud of has been the biggest inspiration to write this book. I want to start with that story because I think its my greatest credibility for everything I'm about to say...

THE FIFTH BROTHER

I never really cared for Leonardo. He was my least favorite of the Teenage Mutant Ninja Turtles. Who appointed him group leader? The one year I asked for a Ninja Turtle costume for halloween, the only one they made at the time was Leonardo and that's what I got stuck with. I was enraged. Are you fucking *kidding* me? How discriminating and ridiculous to design a costume after the same brother who had already been put on a pedestal? I would have rather been any other turtle but Leonardo. I was never able to relate to him.

I first became a fan of the Ninja Turtles in 1987. I was in first grade, living with my father after a raging shit-storm of a custody battle between my parents. After a year and change of being pulled back and forth, I ended up in the judge's chambers where I was told to choose a parent. It's all mostly a blur now, but I know I chose my father. My two older sisters who I had grown up with went to live with my mother, and so the whole family was separated. I remember blaming myself for abandoning my mother and sisters. I hoped my father and I would develop a strong bond, but we struggled. Having spent the first years of my life connecting with my sisters and a very close female cousin, I didn't have the same natural inclinations my father did, and often sensed disappointment in him which made me question my adequacy as a male.

Incidentally, I had no other sources of male inspiration. I had no brothers and no grandfathers, and I rarely saw my one uncle or male cousins. The closest thing I felt to what I imagined was male companionship I experienced through my love for the Ninja Turtles. They were my four imaginary brothers, and I had a unique connection with each one.

There was Michelangelo. He was charismatic and had lots of heart. He was less threatening than the other brothers, but I liked that because I didn't feel like a very tough kid, myself. Mikey was playful and silly, just like me; the fun, loving brother I never had and so badly wanted. He was the first of the bunch I felt a deep connection with.

About two years later, in early 1990, the first Teenage Mutant Ninja Turtle live action film was released to theaters. I'll never forget the scene when Raphael lost his one of his weapons and said, "Damn!" He cursed! That's so cool! I was a little older now, and felt a strong bond with Raf. He was mysterious, dark, and rebellious - everything I wanted to be. He and I were both angry at the world. He was that older brother I looked up to and wanted to learn from. That same year, I got expelled from Catholic school for disruptive behavior.

When I was around ten or eleven, I started keeping my endeavors with my imaginary brothers a secret, because I knew I would be teased by my peers. I began writing and fantasizing about living in the sewers with them and leaving my current life behind, never looking back. It was around this time my focus shifted to Donatello, and I saw something I never noticed before. Donatello got the least attention and the least screen time of all the turtles. He was kind of a loner and an outcast like I was becoming. I was at the bottom of the social ladder at school. Even unpopular kids picked on me. I had very few friends and was picked last for everything. But, that's okay - Donnie and I could be loners together.

In 1993, after the third film was released, I left the theater grappling with the painful realization that I might be outgrowing my relationship with the turtles. I was growing up and becoming some kind of a young man... not the man I wanted to be and certainly not the man my father hoped I'd be.

A 32-DAY STINT

By 13, things at home were getting ugly. My father ridiculed me, called me names, even spat at me. He told me my mother was a whore and my birth was a mistake. He told me I was nothing. I hated him and I felt powerless. My only defense was to internally reject his character and everything about it... but that only turned out to be more detrimental to my own masculinity.

He eventually got fed up and let my mother take me. Starting a new school was the same shit, different setting – struggling to connect with guys and reinforced feelings of male inadequacy. Oh yeah, and the bullying. I took to self-mutilation as a form of escape. I started with a safety pin and graduated to razors. After that lost its thrill, I moved on to fire. I branded myself and put cigarettes out on my arms. After I developed a tolerance to that, I would eventually just hold a lighter to my arm until I couldn't take the stench of the charred skin. I climbed out of my window at night to go get high with groups of young headbangers, punks and stoners. Some even became close friends. Sometimes I came home on my own, other times the police brought me back after finding me passed out in front of a convenience store.

One time, after having gone missing for days, I decided to show up at my high school and go to class like nothing had happened. I wasn't expecting them to lock me into an office and hold me down so I couldn't escape. Apparently, they were instructed to do so after my mother had informed the school I'd been missing. I tried climbing out a window to avoid facing her, but she turned out to be the least of my problems. An ambulance showed up at my high school and out poured a crew of hospital staff. All I remember is when they secured me in four-point restraints, they strapped me in face up, and I could see the faces of all my classmates and teachers as they watched me get rolled into the ambulance and taken to a mental hospital.

They immediately started me on a pretty heavy dosage of anti-depressants and tranquilizers. I continued to find creative ways to self-mutilate from inside the stark white walls and plexiglass windows. Using my teeth, I managed to put a dime-sized hole in my wrist. Each time I'd hurt myself, I'd end up on a stretcher in restraints with a shot in the ass of some medication that made me a zombie. It became a thrill.

At some point, the nurses determined I was in danger of traumatizing the other patients, so they put me on a management plan. That basically meant that every hour of every day was divided between time spent in the milieu with the other patients and time spent isolated in a room. My management plan became more strict the more I acted up, until I was eventually spending 55 minutes of every hour alone in a room. My apologies to the patient's family that, when using that room for a scheduled visit, closed the door and saw ***"FUCK THIS PLACE"*** scrawled in blood on the wall. I had to make good use of my time somehow. I was eventually confined to the quiet room, a padded room used for interval sessions of aggressive release, where I was under constant supervision. They dragged a mattress in there. I ate my meals in there.

A VIOLENT, NAUSEATING BLOW

My story would have been a lot different if a 32-day stint in a mental hospital brought me to some game-changing revelation about my seemingly non-existent masculinity, but nah, that was just the beginning of my downward spiral. There's a bit more before we hit the turning point. Bear with me.

Upon returning home, I resumed some version of high school through one-on-one tutoring since I was no longer permitted to attend classes with the other students. It didn't last long before I stopped showing up, so they tried home instruction. I still remember seeing my tutor standing on the porch through the glass pane in the door, ringing the bell and knocking several times. I'd watch him from the top of the steps where he couldn't see me, and wait for him to finally leave. I feel shitty thinking about it now. I didn't mean to be a jerk. I just wasn't ready to accept help from anyone.

Two misdemeanors later, I was court ordered to juvie - you know, jail for minors. The courtroom officers turned me around, and I faced my mother and father as they cuffed me then took me off to lockdown. Did you know when you enter a jail or prison, they make you strip, lift your ball sack, squat and cough to see if you tried to sneak anything in up your ass? They don't show that in the procedurals and cop dramas. I'm not sure if they put me on high-risk protective custody because they thought I was a danger to myself or because they thought I'd get eaten alive by the other inmates, but they put me in a cage. There was a mattress and that's it. No light. No toilet. I had to bang on the bars until someone heard me if I needed to piss or shit. They eventually sent me across the street to the youth shelter, the lesser of the two evils. I spent two months there until a spot became available in a rehabilitation group home. That's where I spent the next six months practicing 12-step programs and committing myself to a life of sobriety.

Three weeks after being successfully discharged, the police found me underneath the tarp of a boat in someone's driveway, apparently overdosing on heroin. In the emergency room, I remember seeing my sister fading in and out. She appeared to be at the end of a dark tunnel, shaking me, smiling, saying, "C'mon, Frank. Wake up!" I was told later that the doctors had told my family not to let me nod off, because I would stop breathing. Damn, now I failed at masculinity *and* sobriety. I spent a few days in ICU, then I was sent back to the shelter to rot… literally. I could count on one hand how many times I showered there.

My social worker told me I'd only have to stay in the shelter until a spot opened up for me in a nearby long-term boys home. I had heard stories about this place from the guys in the group home. It had a two-year minimum stay and was no fancy private school. This place is where the *really* bad kids went and the staff were allowed to tackle your ass to the ground if they deemed it "necessary." I did not want to end up there. After a year of mental health centers, hospitals and group homes, I was ready to go home. I was tired of state food, no privacy, carrying my cigarettes under my balls, and blowing the smoke into the vents in the bathrooms. I was tired of all that shit. I wanted my freedom back. It was time to behave.

After almost six months of good behavior, I finally managed to convince my social worker and mother that I didn't need to be put in the boys home, and, as long as they were on board, the judge would let me go home. I was almost a free man. On the big day, I arrived at court excited and confident. It had been a long road and this was the day everything was going to change. I ran up to my mom like an excited little kid and she responded with a hesitant, nervous smile.

"Aren't you happy?" I asked.

She didn't say anything. She took my hand and walked me into a nearby stairwell, sat me on the steps and crouched in front of me. Holding my hand, she pulled up my sleeve, exposing a bandage on my wrist. I had cut myself the day before. I couldn't handle the pressure of pretending everything was okay and convincing everyone around me I was fit to be released back home. Nothing was okay. I was reeling inside and going mad in there. I desperately needed some kind of release, and cutting myself felt like purging. I only told one person… one freaking person.

With my hand in hers, she looked up at me as a pained and apologetic look came over her face. I knew what it meant. The realization that my mother was sending me away hit me in the gut in one violent, nauseating blow and collapsed me into a fetal position. I lost it.

FINALLY, THE TURNING POINT

Well, almost. I had to fuck a bunch of shit up first. C'mon, I was 16, had already spent my last two birthdays locked up in facilities and now I'd spend two more the same way. I was pretty pissed. Enraged actually. Free from care and free from fear... so I flew. No, I mean I *actually* flew… headfirst through a double-paned window. I ran and jumped through it. And it was fucking cathartic.

I broke a few more windows, went AWOL, destroyed their cafeteria, held their principal hostage and intentionally provoked the staff. I got my tooth knocked out and my ribs fractured from some brutal restraints, but it didn't stop my purge. After a year of destroying shit, a new staff member took over the wood shop program where residents were taught basic carpentry. This big, bearded lumberjack made me swing a hammer around and do guy stuff. Guy stuff highlighted my deficiency as a male - the great chasm between where I was and what I thought it meant to be a man. It reminded me of my relationship with my father.

"Hit the nail, Frank."

He showed me, though. He didn't laugh at me, shrug me off or get frustrated when he saw me struggling. No. He took his time, explained himself and showed me over and over again. For some reason, I didn't feel inadequate or embarrassed around him. This guy was different. Then finally... Bam! I'll never forget the feeling of invigoration the first time I sunk a nail in one hit. I swear my masculinity made the coin sound in Super Mario Bros. It was the most unfamiliar yet glorious new feeling, and I loved it. Who was this guy and how did he get me to...? He's an enigma! He had all the qualities I admired in other men. He had size, strength and confidence. He was bold and assertive. He was good at guy stuff. He ticked all those boxes. But wait, he also had patience, humility and compassion. I didn't know men like this existed! I was in awe.

I don't remember what I said that led to the conversation about his tumultuous relationship with his father, but it was the beginning of what felt like my first real male companionship. He and I went on to have many more talks about the parallels in our relationships with our fathers, and how we both yearned for male companionship in our childhoods. For the first time in my life, I felt validated *by* a man and validated *as* a man. He told me two things that I'll never forget because they changed my life and proved to be true over and over again:

"You have the ability to be a great leader."

"You need to forgive your father in order to become the man you want to be."

In August of 1999, after two years of being a resident, I was successfully discharged and went back home.

NURTURING DORMANT MASCULINITY

I believe all men have the seed of masculinity. I believe we're all born with an inner *beast* if you will. You, too. It's a nature-*and*-nurture theory. If our environment nurtures that natural seed, it grows, developing into attributes. Without the necessary environment, the seed remains dormant... like mine was. Eventually it grew, but I had to hit rock bottom, almost dying along the way and destroying everything in my path. It wasn't until I met someone who was somehow able to penetrate to my core and validate everything I'd been feeling that I was able to nurture the seed and get a peek at the man I could become. That was the starting point of my masculinity. My goal is to give ***you*** a starting point. I want to penetrate to your core and nurture the seed if it hasn't yet been nurtured. I want to empower you and let you know that you might have something in you that's waiting to be called upon... something you may have doubted exists but yearned for... something that could neutralize those feelings of inadequacy and finally close the self-created, loathsome, shame-inducing, seemingly impassable fucking gap between the man you see yourself as and the man you want to be.

1997

2022

NOTES

NOTES

CRAFTING

MASCULINITY

Ch 2: What is Masculinity?

I make a lot of men question their masculinity.

It's not because I race cars, shoot guns, power lift or "fuck mad bitches." It's because I'm confident and comfortable in my own skin, and that can't really be faked. They see that I know who I am, that I don't feel like I need to prove anything to them, that I don't put on a fake voice, wrinkle my brow, puff out my chest or do any of the common things men do in the presence of other men. I can look them in the eye and ease into being myself - something a lot of men have difficulty doing.

He has a confidence I don't. Does that make him more of a man than me??? Only they can answer that. These guys usually respect me, are intimidated by me, or fucking hate me… or some combination of the three. I used to hate guys like me. Their sole existence would set off my feelings of inadequacy and make me like myself less. Who wouldn't hate and envy that kind of power? Truth is it's easier to learn to like football, race cars, speak in a monotone voice, sleep with a bunch of women and even deadlift 500lbs - some men's notion of what epitomizes masculinity - than it is to develop authenticity and confidence that emanates from the core with ease and undeniable conviction. The latter takes inner work which is often a man's greatest fear. It takes facing certain truths. It takes self-acceptance. It takes balls. This is the kind of masculinity I wanted for myself. The kind that is not only identifiable externally, but internally grounded in truth. To me, all the other stuff is an approximation - an assumption - if there's no inner truth to which it can attach itself.

THE IMPORTANT QUESTION

masculinity:
qualities or attributes regarded as characteristic of men…

There's only one word in this definition, other than conjunctions and prepositions, that is fixed and unquestionable: men. Everything else is at least somewhat subjective. The term *masculinity* refers to men and absolutely nothing else which means it could mean anything... and thus also means nothing. I'm not writing a book that answers the question *what?* Many men and women, some for whom I have great respect, have tried to answer the question *what is masculinity?* You can spend your life trying to turn something gray into black and white, but you'll probably end up negotiating your own biases somewhere along the way. I want to answer the question *how?* How can a man develop his masculinity to be the man he's always wanted to be... *today*?

Granted, we cannot answer *how* without first answering *what*, so now you know this book is inevitably sourced in some bias; mine and that of a lot of other men. Additionally sourced in some biology, sociology, history, my coaching work, and my own personal grapple with yearning for, discovering, and embracing my own ideas of what it means to be a man, I have come up with an applicable method to achieve a collection of qualities commonly sought by men that, together, create a characterization of something I believe is actually attainable:

Mascu*fucking*linity and all it's subjective glory.

So, let's reframe the question. I want you to start thinking about a more important question: what is masculinity to *you*?

Too abstract? Okay. Let's break it down into something even more specific: What qualities do you admire or envy in other men and wish you had but don't know how to attain? If that question gave you a jolt of discomfort, you're probably reading the right book.

AN AUTOBIOGRAPHICAL HOW-TO GUIDE

There is no perfect method for crafting masculinity or any kind of self-development for that matter. If you are looking for a perfect method that can be applied to all men, look in the fantasy section of the library, because it certainly doesn't exist in science, psychology or self-help. We're not baking a fucking cake here. We're dealing with the most abstract and gray areas of life. This book is my personal formula. Each chapter is a summarization of a component of masculinity that I have worked on myself or helped other men develop. Besides the chapter title, I've also included the standout virtue or quality covered in that chapter.

Some chapters will elicit an internal process and others will be more methodical, requiring pen and paper or even physical exercise. This is a handbook. That means there's going to be work involved, starting as soon as the next chapter. For your initial read, I recommend reading the chapters in order, keeping a consistent pace, and reading for enjoyment and insight. Afterward, you can go back and spend extra time on the sections that resonate with you the most. Every one of these chapters has books of information written about its content. Every section of each chapter probably has books of information written about its contents, also. There's plenty more to learn and explore after my book, and I recommend you be diligent in exploring the areas you want to develop the most. It could take a lifetime to master every component of masculinity I touch on. I certainly haven't. This book can be the starting point to the journey.

Because this book is made up of probably 75% of my personal process and successes, with 25% of what I've learned through coaching and research, it has a kind of autobiographical vibe to it. While expression is a passion of mine, I'm driven by a need to develop strategies and applicable solutions, so I had to find that balance in my writing. As self-indulgent and fun as it would have been to simply detail my life story and talk about me the whole time, I wanted to give men something they could use as a resource in life; something they can pick up years after their initial read and say "I need to revisit the chapter on ..." and flip right to it without the need to reread the whole book.

THIS BOOK IS FOR MEN, BUT...

I invite everyone to read it. I believe that men and women are always different by nature and often different by nurture. That said, I do not believe we're opposites and I have no intention to separate us any further. Deducing that something I believe to be a desirable quality in a man must mean I believe is undesirable in, unattainable by, or opposite of a woman is problematic thinking that perpetuates division... and it's bullshit. I hereby revoke your right to draw those conclusions about me.

Men and women are both human and therefore similar, however, while we may all be happier in a world where we never acknowledge our differences or eventually there were no differences, the world we live in today constantly highlights our differences. There are people out there trying to create a more progressive society, and I respect their purpose to better humanity, but there are just as many out there, if not more, perpetuating social constructs. The way I see it is men's and women's experiences are still different enough that it makes sense to acknowledge and discuss the challenges that arise from those experiences. Men, as I discuss them in this book and for those who identity with the term, have it tough in today's society, and I want to empower them. In order to do that, I'll be acknowledging certain social constructs throughout the book. I'm going to refer to men throughout this book and use male pronouns. I do not get into male roles such as husband, father, brother and so on. I do not believe they are a part of masculinity; I believe crafting healthy masculinity can help build a strong foundation for them.

I hope this book lands in the hands of someone who feels similar to how I felt growing up and needs a bearded lumberjack to come validate their story. In most cases, I reckon that's going to be others who identify as male, but virtually everything I discuss in this book can benefit anyone regardless of gender identity. So, I invite ***you*** to read it.

A VIRTUOUS DICKHEAD

I did my damnedest to write this book in a way that does not perpetuate inflexible societal ideology, but acknowledges the ideals with which many of us grew up, and presents them in a way that allows the reader to see the positive qualities underneath the idealized behaviors so he can apply them to himself in a way that is healthy and authentic. This book is about showing you how to be the man *you* have always wanted to be, whether or not it meets someone's standard of a virtuous man, a macho dickhead, or a virtuous dickhead. Whatever. Some folks may argue it's irresponsible of me to write a book that's potentially going to breed more assholes. My rebuttal is this book will not create something that isn't already there and I have no intention to save the world. I just want to make a few men happy and maybe save a few lives. For someone out there, this book is going to be the reason why they stop looking at other men and feeling inadequate. I'm good with that.

Let's get started.

NOTES

NOTES

CRAFTING

MASCULINITY

Ch3: Building an Identity

(self-worth)

Self-worth is the heart of my masculinity. So many of the qualities I see the men I coach admiring in other men are rooted in self-worth: confidence (I am enough), strength (I am able), self-respect (I am deserving) and so on. Self-worth is the foundation I try to build upon to help them become the men they want to be. Without it, where is the truth to attach all the other stuff we want to add on later? That is one of the major differences I see between what I believe is authentic masculinity and pretending, which you may have already learned can be exhausting and unsustainable. Yes, this whole book will hopefully build your self-worth, but it makes sense to start by having some for the other stuff to adhere better. The good news is you do already have worth, but if you're not aware of it, we need to turn it into *self*-worth by helping *you* see it and believe it.

First, let's break down *worth*. In a nutshell, worth is the level at which someone or something deserves to be valued. Well, with people that can be quite subjective, so let's take a look at how it applies to things or products. Besides monetary value, how do we usually determine the worth of something? By giving it an *identity* by answering these three questions:

What is it able to do?
How efficient is it?
Why is it needed?

This is how many of us shop, consciously or subconsciously, and how any good salesman sells a product. The same can be applied to a person. By knowing our identity, we validate ourselves. We give ourselves worth, which then turns into self-worth. Here's what those three questions would look like when applied to you:

What are your strengths?
How aligned are you with your values?
Do you have a purpose?

Strengths + Values + Purpose = Identity.

I believe building an identity for ourselves is the key to our self-worth. Answering this fairly simple equation takes self-reflection and digging into the core, but it's an empowering process. Before I take you through the steps to identifying these three components, we're going to dive a little deeper into understanding what they mean and why each one is a key player in our identity and self-worth.

Strengths. Most of us have never done a truly comprehensive assessment of our character strengths in our adult lives so we don't know them or can't distill them down to simple words. I believe character strengths are the foundation of self-confidence, which is easily the most sought-after personal attribute by the men I have met. For me, this makes it an essential part of crafting masculinity.

Character strengths are a mix of our natural skills, learned skills, and values. They are the root of our potential and abilities, and we all have them. They are largely responsible for the quality of work we generate, and they give us the ability to choose the right hobbies and passions for ourselves. Besides being instrumental in succeeding professional, they also have a direct effect on how successful our personal relationships are.

Identifying character strengths ends up being a favorite for a lot of my guys. Some feel empowered right off the bat and others are initially uncomfortable, feeling like it's self-indulgent and immodest to put so much focus on their own abilities. That's when I jump out of my chair and yell, "Nonsense! That's a story someone told you. A self-judgment. Get it out of your head right now!" Same goes for you. I urge you to give yourself permission to fully embrace your greatness with no guilt or shame. You are great, you have talents and abilities, and you can make it your personal responsibility to yourself and the world to know your character strengths and utilize them as efficiently as possible.

Values. Like character strengths, most guys know they have personal values but just can't identify them or pin them down to specific words. However, if you respect men who are decisive, who have a clear path and seem deliberate in all of their actions, who efficiently prioritize their time and who they spend it with, who exude a sense of certainty and being in control, it's probably because they know their values like the back of their hand. Values help us live our life efficiently.

Personal values are quite simply the things in life that are important to us and have meaning to us. Defining them gives us the ability to make informed, confident decisions and set the right goals for ourselves. The clearer we are on our values, the more purposefully we can live life and do the things we love. The more we do the things we love, the happier we are. It's pretty straightforward.

One of my personal favorite things about values is there is no right or wrong. They're not to be confused with morals, principles, ethics or any system of belief. They are not universal. Values are personal... ours only... rooted exclusively in our thoughts and feelings! Unlike character strengths that tend to change less, values can fluctuate quite a bit throughout our lives. You may find yourself reassessing them every six months or year to ensure your actions stay aligned with what's most important to the most current you.

I often see a major shift in men after we've identified their personal values. I see them begin to develop clarity. I see an increased self-awareness. I see them begin to add and remove people and things from their life as they strive for alignment... it's inspiring! I wish I had identified mine sooner. So many times in life when I was conflicted or at a crossroad, let some fleeting feeling guide me to a decision or betrayed my true self because of a clouded perspective, my values would have put me back on my path. I refer to them often now and I reckon you will, too.

Purpose. Knowing our purpose answers the question "Why am I here?" or "Why am I needed?" or "What's the fucking point?" It makes our day-to-day life feel meaningful and ignites a fire in us. I believe that middle adulthood is where we naturally seek a sense of purpose. It's at that stage, I've noticed men seem to develop a desire to contribute, produce or generate something of lasting benefit for the next generation or longer. I subscribe to the philosophy that doing so, combined with doing things we love, is a key formula to feeling whole. Recent beliefs on how we achieve and sustain happiness and wellness tend to emphasize the importance of these two components as well.

This is where **Strengths**, **Values**, and **Purpose** all come together. Your strengths can lead you to generate or produce something of lasting benefit, and your values can lead you to living a life doing things you love. Combining them can lead you to purpose or *purposeful work* that gives your life more meaning.

Purposeful work does not necessarily mean career path or your 9-5. You probably already have one that you don't intend to change and that's okay. Purposeful work simply means doing something purposeful. It doesn't even have to be a job at all. It can be building Lego houses with your kid if it strengthens your relationship or imparts a lesson. I do not believe our day job has to be our most purposeful work in life. It just needs to afford us a lifestyle that supports our purposeful work. Later in the chapter, I'll detail the specific formula I use to help guys identify their purposeful work and small feasible steps. These are things you can start doing right away (in addition to a job).

Strengths, **Values** and **Purpose** are a powerful trio that have been instrumental in my work. They've helped a lot of men build an identity and increase their self-worth. In the remainder of this chapter, I have outlined the steps I use to identify all three. This is important foundation work but also one of the most dense sections of the book. I usually spend a solid two to three hours on each assessment with the men I work with. The more time you invest, the more impact it will likely have on your self-worth. You do not have to do it right now! Do not let it overwhelm you and do not fret over it. If you're sitting on the toilet or reading under a nightlight at three in the morning, now is probably not the ideal time and that's cool. As I mentioned earlier, you can simply read through it for enjoyment and insight this round. Come back later, or after you've finished the book, for a more in-depth assessment on your own or with a coach.

IDENTIFY YOUR STRENGTHS

Start by thinking about the times in your life when you've felt the strongest. Ask yourself the following questions:

When have I felt the most proud?
What have been my biggest accomplishments?
When have I felt the most challenged?

Once you have some specific situations in mind, try to generate the feeling it gave you by daydreaming about it. Who were you with? What were your surroundings? What was the temperature like? The more details you have, the better you'll be able to play it back in your mind.

Assess your strengths. Play back one situation at a time until you feel you've emotionally reconnected to it. Try to think of the strengths you exhibited that made you feel proud, that led to that accomplishment, or that helped you overcome that challenge. Describe those strengths as best you can and get them down somewhere in a list. Don't worry about being perfect in your descriptions or the order. Just get it down for now. You can use the Values in Action (VIA) framework of character strengths (Peterson & Seligman, 2004) at the end of this section as a reference. Do this for each scenario until you have 10 strengths listed.

This might take a few tries. You may draw a blank initially, and that's okay. If you're not reflective on a regular basis, you need to allow some time to warm up that muscle. Keep those three questions in the forefront of your mind as you go through your day. Things will eventually come to you. Have a place to jot them down in the moment so you don't forget them later. Once you've compiled what you feel is the best list you can produce, set it aside. That's *your* assessment of your strengths. Let's see how it aligns with what other people think of you.

Gather feedback. For this part, you will need to ask 7-10 people you trust to give you feedback. Try to choose people from different areas of your life: family, social, work, and so on. We want to build a list from people who have experienced all sides of you. You can ask your mom, a childhood friend, a boss, an employee, a significant other or ex, a classmate - the more ground you cover, the better. Try to get both male and female perspectives. Ask them to send you what they think are your top 7-10 strengths. Tell them it can be a list of words or it can be sentences. I know this might be uncomfortable. I have literally had guys in tears at the thought of asking other people for what seems like praise and compliments. That is not what you're doing here. Here's how I tell them to frame it:

"Hey, I could use your feedback! I've recently started working on some self-development stuff. Part of my process is to identify my strengths by seeking feedback from 7-10 people in my life who know me the best and for whom I have great trust and respect. You are one of those people! Would you be willing to send me 7-10 things that *you* think are my greatest strengths? I'd be more than happy to do the same for you in return if you're interested. Thanks!"

Doing the same in return is an act of shared vulnerability, and can bring you closer. Once you've collected the strengths from everyone, create a new list and, starting at the top, write the strength that is repeated the most, then second most and so on. Pay attention to the top four. These are the top four strengths that people see in you. Do any surprise you? Is it consistent with how you see yourself?

Find the parallels. Put your own list of strengths next to the combined list of other's assessments of your strengths. Are there parallels? Is there anything mentioned that you didn't see in yourself? Does anything surprise you? Is there anything on your list that no one else mentioned? Maybe it's a hidden strength that no one else has seen.

Build a final list of 10 strengths using both lists. The order is entirely up to you. You decide because you know *you* better than anyone else. Pay attention to the strengths that are repeated the most. Maybe you'll put those at the top. Be honest with yourself and use your best judgment. Highlight the top four. Those are your greatest character strengths. Congratulations on identifying them. Memorize them. Look them over several times, write them down in different places and store them in a place where you can see them daily. One by one, say out loud, "I am _____." Own it.

Let it make you feel something.

VIA 24 CHARACTER STRENGTHS

Wisdom Strengths:
Creativity
Curiosity
Judgment
Love of Learning
Perspective

Courage Strengths:
Bravery
Perseverance
Honesty
Zest

Humanity Strengths:
Love
Kindness
Social Intelligence

Justice Strengths:
Teamwork
Fairness
Leadership

Temperance Strengths:
Forgiveness
Humility
Prudence
Self-Regulation

Transcendence Strengths:
Appreciation of Beauty
Gratitude
Hope
Humor
Spirituality

IDENTIFY YOUR VALUES

Similar to identifying your character strengths, you need to get yourself emotionally reconnected to some of the most impactful times in your life. Ask yourself these questions:

What was the happiest moment(s) of my life?
When have I felt the most proud?
When have I felt the most fulfilled?

Go with your gut. Once you've fully reconnected to those times, you should be feeling nostalgic and quite good. In your current state of tingly-good nostalgia, go through the list of values at the end of this section and start writing or typing the words that resonate with you the most. Follow your gut response. You're going to connect to a lot of words. Trust your instincts and get them all down!

Combine synonymous values. You will probably have a lot of words in front of you that are important to you, but you can't live by all of those words. You need to gradually narrow the list down to something you can memorize. Start by eliminating some of the synonyms. For example, if you wrote *accomplishment, achievement* and *success*, choose one. Another example would be *compassion, sensitivity* and *feelings.* While the words are not exact synonyms, they are similar. Keep the one that resonates with you the most and eliminate the other two. Remember, this is not about what you think is the right answer. Let go of any self-judgment and listen to your gut. If you need to keep a few synonyms on your list for now, it's okay. Get it down to 25 words. This part will take a little longer as you'll want to spend some time with each word and determine what it means to you.

Combine analogous values. You have a list of 25 words that are all probably very important to you. Save this list if you like, because you're about to make an even smaller list. Look for words that are analogous or complimentary and try to combine them. For example, if you have *strength, confidence* and *health* in your list, ask yourself if living out one of them will require you to live out the others. In my case, I decided that *strength* resonates with me most, and in order to live a life that aligns with the value of strength, I'd need to be both confident and healthy. Therefore, I removed *confidence* and *health* from my list. Do the same with the remainder of the words on your list until you have 10. Take your time here.

Once you get your list down to 10 values, put them in order starting with the value that speaks to you the most. You may change the order a few times here. That's okay. A lot of guys find this part the most difficult. If you're really struggling, try asking yourself what values would matter to you the most if you had six months left to live. Once you feel good about your order, highlight the top four. Those are your top four values in life. Make sure you see them somewhere daily. Say them out loud regularly. Memorize them.

Pat yourself on the back. You just gave yourself the ability to set clearer goals, make more informed decisions and live your life with a deeper sense of purpose. Nice.

200+ PERSONAL VALUES

Acceptance
Accomplishment
Accountability
Accuracy
Achievement
Adaptability
Alertness
Altruism
Ambition
Amusement
Assertiveness
Attentiveness
Authenticity
Awareness
Balance
Beauty
Boldness
Bravery
Brilliance
Calm
Candor
Capability
Care
Certainty
Challenge
Charity
Cleanliness
Clarity
Cleverness
Comfort
Commitment
Common sense
Communication
Community
Compassion
Competence
Concentration
Confidence
Connection
Consciousness
Consistency
Contentment
Contribution
Control
Conviction
Cooperation
Courage
Courtesy
Creativity
Credibility
Curiosity
Decisiveness
Dedication
Dependability
Determination
Development
Devotion
Dignity
Discipline
Discovery
Drive
Eclecticism
Effectiveness
Efficiency
Empathy
Empowerment
Endurance
Energy
Enjoyment
Enthusiasm
Equality
Ethicality
Excellence
Experience
Exploration
Expressiveness
Fairness
Family
Fame
Fearlessness
Feeling
Ferociousness
Fidelity
Focus
Foresight
Fortitude
Freedom
Friendship
Fun
Generosity
Genius
Giving
Goodness
Grace
Gratitude
Greatness
Growth
Happiness
Hard work
Harmony
Health
Honesty
Honor
Hope
Humbleness
Humility
Imagination
Impact

VALUES *(cont.)*

Improvement
Independence
Individuality
Influence
Ingenuity
Innovation
Inquisitiveness
Insight
Inspiration
Integrity
Intelligence
Intensity
Intuition
Irreverence
Joy
Justice
Kindness
Knowledge
Leadership
Learning
Liberty
Logic
Love
Loyalty
Mastery
Maturity
Meaning
Moderation
Motivation
Openness
Optimism
Order
Organization
Originality
Passion
Patience
Peace
Performance
Persistence
Playfulness
Pleasure
Poise
Popularity
Potential
Power
Presence
Productivity
Professionalism
Prosperity
Purpose
Quality
Reality
Reason
Recognition
Recreation
Reflection
Respect
Responsibility
Restraint
Results
Reverence
Risk
Sacrifice
Satisfaction
Security
Self-reliance
Sensitivity
Serenity
Service
Sharing
Significance
Simplicity
Sincerity
Skill
Solitude
Spirituality
Spontaneity
Stability
Status
Strength
Structure
Success
Support
Talent
Teamwork
Temperance
Thoughtfulness
Timeliness
Tolerance
Toughness
Tradition
Tranquility
Transparency
Trust
Truth
Understanding
Uniqueness
Victory
Virility
Vision
Vitality
Wealth
Wisdom
Wittiness
Zest

IDENTIFY YOUR PURPOSE

Combining your strengths and values can help you determine what kind of work will bring you the greatest sense of purpose. It's easy in concept, but requires creative thinking. I like to use personality archetypes for some inspiration here. Whether it's Myers Briggs, the zodiac signs, the ninja turtles or the seven dwarfs, it doesn't matter. Archetypes are not absolute in my opinion. They're not hard labels. It's about identifying with an archetype and exploring the strengths, challenges and inclinations of that archetype to see what aligns with your own strengths and values. It can help you realize your potential, peer into sides of yourself you have not yet explored and even recognize shortcomings you may have not worked on otherwise. When you find an archetype you identify with, look at the kinds of work that's most suited for that archetype and see if anything inspires you or feels like a good fit. My favorite model is currently the *Seven Soul Types* from *Michael Teachings.* I identify with more than one archetype depending on different combinations of my strengths and values. You might, too.

Find feasible steps. Using the sample sentence below as a template, add in your own *strength, value, purposeful work,* and *small feasible step* in that order. You can use your favorite archetype model or your creativity to come up with purposeful work that makes sense for the corresponding strength and value combination. Next try to find a small feasible step that you could start doing with reasonable ease. This requires a lot of brainstorming and takes time. Start with just a few and do more if you feel inspired. There are 16 possible combinations of strengths and values. If you're up for it, try them all.

With my strength of *empathy* and my value of *greatness,* I'd find purpose in *leadership* by *starting a motivational blog for men.*

Find what moves you. Go through all of your sentences and read them aloud. Try to imagine yourself doing them. Which ones excite you? Which ones energize you? Which ones would you do for free? Which ones would you do if you had a year left to live? The ones that make you really feel something are the ones to which you need to pay the most attention. Those are the ones that have potential to give you purpose.

Small steps only. Remember, if you're just getting started on your journey, you're probably going to make a lot more discoveries as you read, and you may not want to overwhelm yourself with any major life changes yet. You *can* start taking action on some of the small steps you've found, however. Every little action counts and leads to big changes. We will delve further into implementation later on. Right now, let yourself get excited that you have developed a deeper understanding of your purpose.

Bravo! As I mentioned earlier, this is one of the densest chapters and requires a lot of patience, diligence and reflection. Nonetheless, I feel it's a critical starting point for the journey. Do you feel more confident after identifying your character strengths? Do you feel a deeper sense of clarity after identifying your personal values? Do you feel more passion after determining your purposeful work? If you don't feel any changes, don't be mad at yourself, don't judge yourself and don't toss out the book just yet. Sometimes inner change is a slow burn. Self-worth takes time and often others will see it in us before we notice it in ourselves. Be patient. Most people never do this kind of self-work in their adult life. They don't make the time for it, don't know what steps to take or the emotional fatigue becomes too great and they throw in the towel. Taking the time to do this for yourself is already a testament of self-worth, self-respect and self-love.

NOTES

NOTES

CRAFTING

MASCULINITY

Ch4: Braving Fears

(courage)

Sometimes I feel like the world is full of a bunch of fucking cowards. It's as though men are always scared of something. Well, fear is all throughout our circuitry, informing our behaviors and choices, and protecting us from danger. It's also largely responsible for humanity surviving as long as it has. The biochemical response to fear, to fight or flight, is what kept our ancestors alive. If fear is an inherent part of humanity, does that make all men wimps? No. I think it's fair to conclude we have little control over our biochemical responses, but what happens next is totally personalized and how we deal with those feelings could be a testament of our character as a man.

Fear is a complex and intense emotion and we all feel it. It can be paralyzing or thrilling, but it all comes down to danger in one way or another. Whether we're on a rollercoaster, living through a pandemic, watching a scary movie, falling hopelessly in love, preparing for a job interview or coming face to face with the beast we need to kill to feed our family, fear is generated by the brain's detection of perceived danger. What does the brain perceive as danger? Basically, anything that's associated with a past emotional trauma or negative experience, anything that can lead to physical pain or illness, anything that makes us feel a lack of control and ultimately anything unfamiliar to us. Do you see the problem? Fear is constantly set off erroneously by these subconscious associations when there is no real danger present. In serving to protect us and keep us safe, fear can consequently block us from living a fulfilling life and from taking risks. This is what psychologists like to call irrational fear.

(Enter courage)

Contrary to what many believe, courage is not the absence of fear. In fact, courage is not a feeling at all. It's an ability, a strength and a value that we can call upon in the face of fear.

Without fear, there is no courage. They go hand in hand. Too often I see guys shrinking in the face of fear because they claim they didn't feel courage. You're not going to *feel* courage! You might feel confident when fear is present or you might feel determined, which can support an act of courage, but the only feeling you really need to identify in order to be courageous is fear, itself. Then, after rationalizing whether or not the fear is rooted in any real danger, you're left with a choice of action. It is in these times we feel the most defeated, choked and obstructed that we are gifted with an opportunity to prove to ourselves how strong we are. We can choose to start seeing these moments as a critical time to grow our self-worth when it's the most susceptible to grow. It's like a flower waiting to be pollinated by an act of courage and the seed it produces is confidence.

I was tired of living my life in fear. It was when I realized that confidence is not a requirement for a courageous act, but a reward for it that my life began to change. It was scary as shit in the beginning, but it got easier as my confidence grew. After just *one* courageous act, courage went from being what seemed an impossible task to a really difficult-but-doable one. Little by little, through more of these acts, courage became easier to call upon. Eventually it became one of my greatest strengths and values as a man, and confidence was the byproduct. In this chapter, I'm going to tell you how I did that.

WEAK MEN SELDOM FAIL

...because they seldom take risks. The first step to courage is a willingness to fail. You have to be willing to fall flat on your face. This is the scariest thing for some men, especially those whose greatest values are acceptance, appearance, popularity or status. Failure is essential for growing and building our character. It is not bad. It's not a lack of success and it's not a testament of our strength. It's how we respond to failure that is a measure of our character. Failing builds our toughness and resilience. Men who fail repeatedly develop perseverance and determination in the face of adversity. What'll happen if you continue to live your life playing it safe?

Do you never want to leave your comfort zone?
Do you never want to know your full potential?
Do you never want to perform well in difficult situations?
Do you never want to stand out?

You didn't pick up this book to remain stagnant. Say this out loud: "I am going to fail as often as necessary, and to do that, I am going to start taking well-assessed and calculated risks." Boom. You just put that into the universe.

Taking risks is not always about succeeding. In fact, if you're doing it as part of your self-development, the result has no bearing on it whatsoever. Once you have measured the risk and determined that a failure is not insurmountable, taking it becomes about the process of braving your fears to become a stronger, more confident man. Look for opportunities to take risks in your social life, career, student life, fitness and wherever other opportunity presents itself.

Measure the risk. Be objective here. Ask yourself honestly what could possibly go wrong and measure the consequence of failure objectively, not emotionally. For example, if you are thinking of speaking publicly or presenting something in class or at work, you might identify stumbling on your words as a possible risk. So then what would happen? You might feel embarrassed. Lean into the discomfort that comes up when you think about how that will feel. Now ask yourself what else could happen. Will you be removed from the establishment, shunned, kicked out of class or fired? Will it ruin any relationships? Will it destroy your fucking life? No? Then it's probably a risk worth taking.

Only you decide what risks you take. No one else. That means no one else should discourage you from taking a risk you have already measured and decided you want to take, and no one should pressure you into taking a risk you have objectively determined is not worth taking.

Find your courage. Remember your strengths. Go over them in your head and remind yourself that you are strong and no matter how this goes, you're going to be fine. Affirm to yourself that you only have something to gain here, even if you fail. An undesired outcome is not a testament of your worth; you're a great guy. It's not a testament of your overall competence; you have skills and talents and you know that. Make a promise to yourself that regardless of the result, you are going to reward yourself afterward for your efforts. You are going to bounce back despite any feelings of defeat or discouragement. You are going to be okay... no matter what!

Fuck what anyone else thinks. You are doing this for yourself and no one else. It does not matter who you disappoint and what anyone else thinks of you afterward. You need to trust yourself. If you know you want to take the risk after properly assessing it, you do not need to justify it to anyone else. That means friends, relatives, and especially parents. Parents, especially mothers, often have an instinct to protect us. Fathers sometimes have an instinct to pressure us into being the man they want us to be. Let go of all of that shit. You are your own man and you make your own decisions.

Fuck what everyone else thinks or what they're going to think. Do this because *you* want to.

Some ways to take risks:

- Tell someone you like them
- Quit a job you don't like and don't need
- Speak publicly
- Go first
- Disagree with a teacher
- Travel alone
- Share something you created
- Take a physical challenge
- Speak to a stranger
- Do something you suck at
- Apologize
- Negotiate something
- Thank someone or give them praise
- Do something that makes you uncomfortable
- Let someone interview you on their podcast
- Make a "How to" video and share it
- Write an e-book
- Openly admit to a flaw or fear
- Apply for a job you think you won't get
- Sing karaoke sober
- Ask for more money
- End an expired friendship
- Take an improv class

IN A WORLD OF MASKS, GO UNMASKED

Be authentic. In the beginning of the book, I mentioned that I make a lot of men question their masculinity, and not because I race cars, shoot guns, power lift or fuck a bunch of women. It's because I'm authentic. My masculinity is authentic. Men see that I know who I am, and that I don't feel like I need to prove anything to them or try to impress them. I can look them in the eye and be myself with ease. That's authenticity.

A lot of guys can learn to benchpress an impressive amount of weight through diligence, but it takes courage to lead with your most authentic self. It takes inner work and facing certain truths. It takes balls. For me, authenticity is the boss and the other stuff is just add-ons.

Put a little star next to this section in the book. It could have had its own chapter. It could have been its own book, even. I want to emphasize how important authenticity is and how much it will make you unique from the majority of the men around you. By reading this book, building your worth, your identity and working on yourself from a place of honesty, courage and acceptance, you are already building your authenticity. You are facing and embracing truths about yourself - accepting the ones you don't love and optimizing the ones you do. You are already on the path to living as your most unmasked self. Because I love authenticity so much, I still wanted to give it a section to point out a few things that'll help you get there faster.

Give up the need to be liked. Focusing on being liked will compromise your authenticity, take the focus off the task at hand, raise the stakes of a situation unnecessarily and ultimately have a negative effect on your behaviors, performance and growth. Your driving force will be to impress others or earn their acceptance or praise which can cause you to betray your values. Making other's opinions less important to you will keep you grounded in your ability to act without any unnecessary, self-generated obstacles or distractions. When I stopped caring so much about being liked, I gained more clarity. It got me out of my head and put the focus back on my values, objective, or whatever the task at hand was. When my focus was in the right place, people actually started liking me more. It was as if making them less important gained more of their respect. I no longer seemed desperate for their approval. It didn't look like I was trying so hard. And that made people flock to me. Sure, a few envious people liked me less due to my confidence… but they still respected me. When you become your best self, some folks might feel threatened by you. I learned to accept it. You can, too.

Give up the need to belong. Your vibe attracts your tribe. Not vice versa. Be careful about how much you let a group of guys you desperately want to be accepted or befriended by mold your behaviors and choices. We all want to belong. Nothing wrong with that as long as we find our identity *first*. That'll determine our tribe. If you do it the other way around... blindly searching for your tribe with the hopes that something feels right or that some group you admire will accept you... it'll take a helluva lot longer to find your authenticity. You'll be wasting time molding yourself to conform to whatever tribe has accepted you in an effort to secure your membership. How can you feel like you're a part of something if you're not living as your most authentic self? Your tribe can't define you. It can't give you an identity. That's backwards, man. Your identity is what defines the tribe!

You have to find you *first*.

Give up the need to be superior. Do you make yourself grandiose to other men? Do you minimize them or highlight their flaws, directly or indirectly, as a way to establish your superiority? You might be inauthentically presenting yourself as smarter, stronger, more honorable, or more worthy through the ways you interact with them as a way to mask your own flaws. Do you respond to criticism with humility, or do you instead criticize back and find other ways to reestablish high status?

Men like this are usually surrounded by yes-men and followers rather than men they see as equals. They prefer it that way and most of us just don't want to be around someone who always looks for ways to appear better. These guys are prone to lots of criticism as other men stand by waiting for opportunities to knock them off their high horse. The funny thing is grandiosity often isn't conscious or intentional. When deep down a man believes he needs to be better than other men, it will manifest behaviors that produce it. It can be a tricky thing to discern whether some of the guys around you have a grandiosity complex themselves or if they are responding to yours. By giving up the need to be better and responding to moments of insecurity with humility and a little vulnerability, you'll counter-balance grandiosity in yourself and others, and come across a lot more authentic.

ASSERTIVE MEN FINISH FIRST

This is crucial. I am amazed at how many men are unable to assert themselves. Dude, how much of a man are you really if you push a big truck and have a skull tattoo, but turn completely passive when it comes to an uncomfortable conversation? This is troubling to me. Assertiveness takes courage *and* skill. It's a quality of a dying breed of man, especially when so much of our communication these days happens electronically, making it much easier to dodge, deflect and side-step.

Perhaps if more men understood the benefits of being assertive, they would make more of an effort to work toward it. In short, guys who assert themselves get to the finish line faster and without compromising their self-respect or respect of others. Here are some of the standout ways I've personally grown from learning to be assertive. It helped me

...get what I want.
...get respect from others.
...stop being taken advantage of.
...become a great manager and leader.
...have less stress and anxiety.

Doesn't every man want those things? Each one is an invaluable gem. And we can have them by simply adjusting our communication style? Yes, I believe we can.

Have a look at the four communication styles on the next two pages. Which style do you think you revert to the most? If you think you're mostly passive, your focus might be to accept that confrontation is sometimes a necessary part of life. A difficult conversation might be uncomfortable short-term, but can resolve long-term grief. If you think you are mostly aggressive, your focus might be to learn to keep your weapons in their holsters when they aren't needed. We can express ourselves tactfully and without destroying relationships. If you're mostly passive-aggressive, your focus might be to start saying what you actually mean and taking responsibility for your thoughts, your feelings and your actions.

COMMUNICATION STYLES *

Passive:

Behavior
Don't say what you feel, need or want.
Put yourself down.
Apologize when you express yourself.
Deny that you disagree or feel differently.

Belief
Others' needs are more important than yours.
They have rights; you don't.
Their contributions are valuable and yours are worthless.

Emotion
Fear of rejection.
Helplessness, frustration and anger.
Resentment toward those who use you.
Reduced self-respect.

Goal
Avoid conflict.
Please others at any expense.

Aggressive:

Behavior
Express your feelings and wants as though any other view is stupid or unreasonable.
Dismiss, ignore or insult the feelings and needs and opinions of others.

Belief
Your needs are more important or more justified than theirs.
You have rights; they don't.
Your contributions are valuable; theirs aren't.

Emotion
Angry or powerful in the moment.
Victorious when you win.
Shame, guilt or self-hatred afterward for hurting others.
Regretful.

Goal
Gain control over others.
Win at any expense.

(Continued...)

Passive-Aggressive:

Behavior
Failure to meet the expectation of others through "deniable" means. Forget, delay, make up obstacles. Deny responsibility for your actions.

Belief
You are entitled to get your own way even after making commitments to others. You are not responsible for your actions.

Emotion
Fear that you would be rejected if you were more assertive. Resentment at the demands of others. Fear of confrontation.

Goal
Get your own way without taking any responsibility.

Assertive:

Behavior
Express your feelings, needs and wants directly, honestly and respectfully. Don't assume you're right. Allow others to hold their own views without dismissing them

Belief
Everyone's needs are equally important. Everyone has the right to express themselves. All views are valuable. You take responsibility for your behavior.

Emotion
You feel positive about yourself and the way you treat others. Self-esteem rises.

Goal
All express themselves and keep their self-respect.

** Paterson, Randy J. (2000). The Assertiveness Workbook: How to Express Your Ideas and Stand Up for Yourself J. Gastwirth (Ed.)*

There are a lot of ways assertive communication can be applied. Every book and article you find on it will point out the basic principles of assertiveness and the writer's opinion on how to adhere to them. I'm going to share with you the four major changes I made in my communication style that have made me more assertive and have proven to be useful tools for the men I've coached.

Ask for what you want. It seems reasonable and simple in concept, but it used to terrify me. I used to feel like I was putting somebody out by asking them for something, and so I avoided it. I was more concerned about other people's feelings than my own needs. There was probably also some part of me deep down that felt I didn't deserve what I wanted to ask for and dreaded the likelihood of rejection. Whenever I was able to muster up the courage to ask for something, my pitch was so riddled with doubt, over-explaining and implications that I unknowingly set myself up for the reinforcing "no" that was to follow.

Needless to say, I rarely got my needs met. I've seen this a lot in other men, in both their professional and personal lives. They pile on excuses as to why they shouldn't ask for what they want. My job is to be their advocate and help them see all the reasons they should.

The first step in asking for what you want is convincing yourself that you deserve it. Be your own advocate! You're not going to convince someone else that what you're asking for is reasonable if you don't believe it yourself. Whether you're asking for a raise, more time on a project, a favor from a friend, a dinner date, or a finger up your ass, you better ask for it with conviction.

Sit down and figure out all of the reasons why what you're asking for is reasonable and why you're worth it.

Second, don't beat around the bush. Just ask for it. Implying your needs, being vague about amounts or skipping over important details can read as dishonest or manipulative. There's nothing wrong with feeling out the other person's emotional temperature as you prep them for your ask, but taking 10 minutes to get to the same ask that you could've reached in two minutes didn't make the ask any more palatable for the other person. It simply wasted eight unnecessary minutes of their life. Be direct and get the hard part over with. You can discuss it after.

Third, be careful about piling on too many reasons. This can come across as poor advocation for yourself and like you don't really believe what you're asking for is reasonable. Too many reasons can also sound like an apology. "I'm sorry, I know what I'm asking for is a lot, but here's all of the reasons I've come up with!" You do not need to apologize, literally or behaviorally, when asking for something. It usually means you weren't diligent enough in convincing yourself you deserve what you're asking for. As a default, and this can certainly vary per circumstance, think about emphasizing one main reason why your ask is justified if a reason is needed at all. Then have two other prepared reasons as a backup if more are necessary.

Lastly, prepare in advance for rejection. Going into a situation prepared for the worse possible outcome can lessen the blow if it doesn't go the way you hoped, making for a faster recovery. This is not setting yourself up for failure. You still ask for what you want with confidence and hope for a positive outcome. If anything, the moment before your ask, you might even prep yourself for receiving the positive response you want so you can put yourself in high spirits and self-generate confidence. However, prior to that, imagine how it would feel to get denied and accept it in advance as a way of saying to yourself, "Okay, so that's the worst that can happen and I can handle that."

Set boundaries. This was a game changer for me. I used to be taken advantage of constantly. Looking back, I blame myself for it. Why do I blame me and not the ones who took advantage? Because I trained them how to treat me through my own behaviors and reactions. Humans will be humans. My personal and professional life have shown me that we are opportunists by nature, and most of us will take advantage of a situation when we know we can get away with it. Here are some of the stories humans tell themselves:

I can cancel with him if I need to. *(opportunistic behavior)*
He's understanding. *(justification)*

I don't have to meet deadlines with him. *(opportunistic behavior)*
He always gives more time. *(justification)*

I can tell him to do it if no one else wants to. *(opportunistic behavior)*
He always helps out. *(justification)*

I can talk to him however I want. *(opportunistic behavior)*
He never gets mad. *(justification)*

I can always borrow money from him. *(opportunistic behavior)*
He's very generous. *(justification)*

I can ask him to work Christmas. *(opportunistic behavior)*
He never complains. *(justification)*

Do any of these examples sound like your life? Notice how the justification for *their* opportunistic behaviors are based entirely on *your* behaviors? Busy humans, especially ones in need, can become self-centered and easily convince themselves that you just don't mind being shit on. But you do. Ohhh, you do. Is your resentment bubbling into a rage as you read this? Good. I hope it is. Because this is the end of being taken advantage of. Those days are behind you. You're a new man - one who's no longer afraid to set clear boundaries.

The first step in setting boundaries is to define your limits so you know where to draw the line with people. You'll want to assess the times in your life where you have felt pushed, violated, or taken advantage of in all of your relationships. Consider friends and family, significant others, work peers, bosses, acquaintances and even strangers. Think about the times you've felt resentful or angry toward someone because they crossed a line, albeit one you may not have clearly drawn. Situation by situation, start defining on paper the limits you no longer want to be breached. This will act as a loose guideline to live by that you can adjust appropriately as you evolve. Here's a few examples:

- I want deadlines adhered to by my employees.
- I want my time to be respected by my friends.
- I want to be spoken to respectfully by my boss.
- I will lend money only to family whom I trust.
- I want to always be treated fairly.
- I want to protect myself from abuse.

Once you know your boundaries, it's up to you to enforce them. Otherwise, they mean nothing. You have to act courageously and start saying them. Practice reading them aloud when you're alone if you need to. When you first start setting boundaries, it will feel uncomfortable and out of character. Growing pains, buddy. You have to trust it. Setting boundaries is not mean or selfish, despite what anyone tells you. It is a testament of your self-worth and self-respect, and it shows that you value fairness. It tells people that you expect to be treated a certain way and you will not stand for anything less, even at the expense of losing the relationship. People will respect you. Remember: our behaviors and reactions train people how to treat us.

The funny thing about boundaries is that even though people often do not like when we set them, they usually listen. You may notice when you start drawing lines that some people in your life are taken aback, hurt or offended. People don't like being told *no*, and while a negative response is not the outcome we seek, it's usually a sign we were successful in setting a clear boundary. Focus less on a person's temporary emotional response and more on their future behaviors. Do their behaviors show they've acknowledged the boundary you've set? If so, bravo. If not, tell them a second time, more sternly than the first, but I would not tell them a third time. If someone won't respect your boundaries, feel free to ignore, fire, quit, delete, write off, or do whatever is necessary to ensure the boundaries don't get crossed again.

Say no. It took some time for me to get good at this. As a natural giver, I initially struggled with overwhelming feelings of guilt as I disappointed all of the people in my life who were used to hearing me say *yes*. Saying *no* was painful and it fucked up so many good moments. *No* is inherently negative and rejective. Whether in a professional setting or a personal relationship, nobody responds happily to a rejection. So why would anyone want to ruin a perfectly good mood with negativity? I wanted to be the guy who was liked for his positivity; not the guy who made people feel bad. And let's not leave out the sense of impending doom that came when I knew that my *no* was going to lead to a conflict. Who wants to feel that? Saying *no* sucked.

Well, it sucked short-term. The payoff of saying *no* didn't hit until later... when I was doing the things I wanted to do instead of the things I said I couldn't do... and when the money I said I couldn't lend was spent on something I wanted to spend it on... and when the weekends I said I couldn't work were spent taking care of me. I began to feel less depleted and like I had more left for me. I was happier.

After realizing this long-term payoff of saying *no* was invaluable to me, I started saying it more and more. Over time I discovered that saying *no* didn't only put time and money back in my life, it also taught me to put me first. It tested the integrity of my relationships. It gained me respect. It gave me confidence. Who knew *no* could be so fucking powerful? I started saying that shit like it was going out of style.

"No, no, no, no, NO!"

No is one of the most powerful weapons to shield the perimeter of you and yet so many men struggle to say it. It gives you control in your life and keeps you aligned with your values and goals. In your relationships, it will help you discern who loves you from who wants to control you. It will guard you from being taken advantage of or exploited.

Saying *no* is assertive and an act of courage, and you can use it as often as it suits your needs. There's a nice gray area between self-*care* and self*ish*, and you get to decide where you want to live on that spectrum. The sacrifices you make are your choice. Make them because they align with your values, not because someone has pressured you or judged you as being rigid. Saying *no* isn't going to make you friends and you're bound to get some pushback, but it is going to make your life better the moment you start saying it.

Saying *no* is also a skill, and you're probably going to be terrible at it in the beginning. That's okay. You'll get better at it, trust me. I'm going to give you a heads up on a few ways to say *no* effectively that I had to learn through trial and error.

First, don't people-please when saying *no*. It really hurts your credibility to soften your *no* so much that it starts to sound like a *maybe* when it never was. Saying *no* now is better than resentment or disappointment later. That means don't smile and say "Okay, I'll think about it" if you are not going to think about it. Granted, that's a baby step of progress from saying *yes* when you didn't mean it, but it's going to lead you to the same place– the inevitable need to eventually say *no*. So, be honest and say what you mean from the start. There is no need to feel guilty or please the other person.

Something else worth mentioning is that ignoring does not replace a *no*. That's a copout. It's cowardly and it's actually more offensive than saying *no*. If you ever find yourself avoiding someone because you think they'll get the hint and deduce that your answer is *no*, smack yourself. This is a terrible habit and it unfortunately happens a lot. Be the one to stop the cycle or at least do it for your own personal growth. Ignoring is not cool and not assertive, but there are a couple exceptions when it might be okay. If it's a situation where you're getting a plethora of messages and you simply can't correspond with each person, such as responses to a dating profile, a job ad, or an audition, nonresponse might be widely understood as a *no*. Another example would be if you have already said *no* more than once and someone persists anyway. A nonresponse might say "the answer hasn't changed." Otherwise, try to steer clear of ignoring or ghosting people. Personally, I have always seen that as immature and, well, unmanly.

I learned the best way to say *no* is to keep it simple. There's no need to pile on reasons and unmask your guilt or discomfort. That will hurt you more than help you by giving the other person an opportunity to challenge your reasons or play on your vulnerabilities. Say it in a way that leaves no room for negotiation unless there *is* room and you want to. In that case, you can say *no* and then provide another option you would be open to. Also, in keeping it simple, a ton of emotion is not necessary.

Trust the words themselves. No means no. The following can also mean no, depending on the circumstance:

- That doesn't work for me.
- I'm not interested.
- I'm okay, thank you.
- I'm going to pass.
- I'd rather not.

Lastly, please be careful with the "it's me, not you" tactic. Personally, I really dislike this tactic, but when done well, it can lessen the blow. When done poorly, it could make the other person feel worse and comes across as pitying and insincere, especially if it's in a dating scenario. Be honest. Making it about you can be as simple as "It's not a good fit for me" or "It's not what I'm looking for right now."

Stop apologizing unless an apology is called for. I'm still working on this one! I have this habit of saying *sorry* in situations that don't call for it in order to verbally make everything okay. For example, let's say I'm walking through a doorway and someone else is attempting to do the same from the opposite direction. No one is in the wrong, but as we dance back and forth in an effort to get out of each other's way, I might smile and say *sorry*. It's not necessary. It can be replaced with *excuse me* or nothing at all. I'm using an apology to make everything okay when I haven't done anything wrong. Language is important to me. I believe it programs our subconscious.

Resolving this is simply about bringing it into my conscious mind and practicing more silence when words are not necessary, or swapping out *sorry* with something else that isn't apologetic. So why haven't I done that yet? Because I have other things I want in my consciousness that are more important for my development, and this usually ends up getting put on the back burner. I'll get to it eventually. I don't want to minimize the importance of it to you, though. If it's something you find yourself doing in the next, more problematic, scenario, then it will be worth your conscious efforts to work on it.

Apologizing isn't always done through the words *I'm sorry.* Sometimes it's in between the lines of what you're saying, and if there's no need for an apology, it can hurt your objective and the outcome. For example, if you notice you have a tendency to pile a bunch of apologetic language onto an ask, practice removing it and see if the ask is just as effective and/or produces a better outcome.

<u>To a superior:</u>
I don't mean to bother you, but *could I trouble you* to schedule a brief meeting to discuss last week's numbers?

<u>To a friend or family:</u>
I know this may sound arduous, but *would you mind* responding to my message today so I can make the reservation?

<u>To a student or employee:</u>
I hope I'm not being too difficult, but I'd really like the reports to be handed in by Friday *if it's not too much of a hassle.*

Everything italicized could be perceived as apologetic and might be unnecessary cushioning. Too much cushioning can weaken your ask, and some folks might see that as a way out. Of course it would be incomplete to deduce that these phrases should never be used. It's circumstantial. If you're interrupting someone, already asked them for several things or know that this ask is going to really put them out, maybe it's a good idea to show some understanding and be more polite. Pay attention to your habits. Take note if you're using apologetic language circumstantially or by default. Consider how these might land more effectively:

To a superior:
1) Can we schedule a meeting to discuss last week's numbers?
2) I'd like to discuss last week's numbers with you, but I see you're busy. Are you able to schedule a brief meeting?

To a friend or family:
1) Could you respond to my message about the reservation?
2) I would like to make the reservation. I understand you are still working out your schedule. Do you think you can respond to my message today?

To a student or employee:
1) Please hand in the reports by Friday.
2) I'd like the reports to be handed in by Friday. I know it's a busy week for everyone. Thank you for your hard work.

The first examples remove the apologetic language and the objective is still the same. There's nothing rude about being direct. The second examples replace the apologetic language with some acknowledgment of the other person's situation. It's polite, but not apologetic. Apologizing softens the objective and hurts your chances of achieving it; acknowledging the other person's feelings and needs shows understanding and consideration but keeps the request strong. The same applies to saying no, addressing an issue, or any other situation where apologetic language isn't called for that you may be misusing it.

ALOOFNESS IS A LAME MOVE

Just a quick side note to address a little habit I've noticed of some men who struggle with assertiveness. Why do so many men resort to acting aloof? It really is a passive move whenever it can be replaced with assertiveness. So why? Well, let's first break down aloofness and where it comes from - it isn't inherently negative.

The term comes from the mid-16th century exclamation "a luff!" Sailors called this out when the ship's head drifted toward the shore, and it essentially means to stay at a distance, move away from or avoid. Today, the term specifically refers to an emotional state. Avoiding danger in life is obviously wise, and there may be times when making yourself emotionally distant will avoid an unnecessary conflict. That's reasonable. However, if you're taking on an aloof emotional state as a way to dodge something that can be addressed head on simply because it makes you squirm, that is the antithesis of authenticity and courage. Knock it off, fellas. While you may have thought it made you seem poised and in control to break out the stone cold, detached demeanor, to anyone with courage you probably looked like a coward. Besides, does that kind of avoidance align with your values? Food for thought the next time you catch yourself misusing aloofness as a solution. Use assertiveness instead!

VULNERABILITY, HA

So many men hate vulnerability – the word, the meaning and the power it has been given. A lot of men cringed when pop psychology tried to redefine a word they've been taught is inherently negative as something entirely different... something positive, even. Here's how I feel about it: the word means the same thing no matter how you slice it. Whether or not it's positive or negative is based entirely on the circumstance and up to you to discern.

Vulnerable – coming from the Latin word, *vulnus,* which means *wound* – means susceptible to physical or emotional attack or harm. That sounds downright negative, doesn't it? Certainly, when faced with an opponent, I'd not want to intentionally make myself vulnerable, but is there ever a time in life when vulnerability can produce a positive outcome? I think so. Say, for example, someone offers their heart to us in the form of a declaration of love or admiration, or sharing something that is intimate to them. How could we respond? We could become suspicious and remain guarded. We could see them as weak. We could also choose to trust and feel honored. We could choose to let their act of vulnerability disarm us as well. Responding with the same vulnerability is one of the ways humans connect, I believe. It's egoless, and, by definition, courageous.

Vulnerability can also be in the form of admitting to an insecurity, weakness, or flaw as I mentioned earlier. In this case, the subjectivity of vulnerability is entirely based on what we see as the danger or harm at stake. If we rationally deduce that there is no real threat of danger, but there is a risk of potential emotional attack, would there be courage in our willingness to endure the potential attack in the name of self-worth? Yes, if we or someone else perceives it that way. Personally, I see this as an important process in the journey to self-worth. Comparatively, projecting invulnerability as a means of masking what we see as a personal weakness when there is no real threat of danger is usually a sign of shame or fear. Keeping it masked guarantees it'll remain a deficiency in our self-worth and is, therefore, a weakness.

Context is everything when it comes to vulnerability. There is strength in keeping ourselves safe from danger and there is also strength in living as our most authentic self by acknowledging and occasionally embracing our squishy, frail guts. It's up to us to discern the difference.

Courage is about facing your fears of failure, rejection, loneliness, pain and so on. It's about taking risks, asserting honesty and leading with your most authentic self even in difficult times. The bravest men faced the beast even if they feared death. Today you hopefully won't be facing any real beasts, so your courage is measured by the times that you are willing to face the modern-day beasts of confrontation, change, vulnerability, pain, adversity, new challenges, and uncharted territories.

Think about small, incremental courageous acts you can start implementing now rather than overburdening yourself with the undertaking of a total character makeover. You don't need to wake up a hero. It's the little things that add up to huge transitions. I've watched it happen right before my eyes. My guys implement small changes, bit by bit, as we talk through them. Over time I see the ways it develops in their confidence and eventually so do the other people around them.

Take small steps and document your progress. After the first one you'll already be braver than you were yesterday.

NOTES

NOTES

CRAFTING

MASCULINITY

Ch5: Solidifying the Body

(presence)

If you think about any men you've admired, you may find that a lot of the masculinity they exude is in their physical presence and movement. It's probably very solid. That's not to say that fluidity or fluid motion is inherently non-masculine. In fact, I think it adds color and rhythm to our movement. I definitely don't want to turn you into a robot- chest puffed out, tension throughout the body, militant walk... you know what I'm talking about. I think we've all seen how that looks. I want to show you ways to develop a firm structure *with* character and personality. That means we start with a rock-solid foundation, then later you can color it with some fluidity for individuality and uniqueness.

This chapter, unlike the last two, is going to elicit an external process for crafting your masculinity. I like working from the inside out and the outside in. Internal work manifests outward, affecting our behavior and physicality. External work uses a different part of the brain, but when practiced diligently, it eventually creates a shift in us psychologically or internally. They are mutually reciprocal processes for self-development.

Our physicality is half our identity. Why don't more people explore it and develop it? Most people, including those who have studied the psychology of body language such as helping professionals, detectives, and athletes, rarely peer deep enough into their *own* physicality to realize we actually have the power to craft and hone our physical identity the way we want. Most people simply accept it as fixed and either carry it around as an insecurity, try to mask it, lean even further into their natural inclinations in an attempt to convince the world they're proud of who they are, or simply throw their hands in the air and say "that's just me." All of that is fine if it works for you. I'm telling you that the same way you can work on your interior self while remaining truthful to who you are, you can also work on your exterior self.

I'm not a chiropractor or physical therapist and this chapter isn't about *correcting* your physicality. This chapter is about honing your physical identity to align with the man you want to be. The insights I share are from the perspective of a performing artist. I spent the better part of a decade studying physical movement and how the physical self relates to the emotional self for the purpose of developing a more specific character. I want to share those insights with you in a way you can apply to crafting and developing your own physical identity. Have fun with these exercises. Learn how to communicate using your body and note how people respond differently. The way I was taught is to start big to create a new habit, then, once it sticks, gradually scale it back to something that feels authentic and sustainable. Pick and choose what works for you. Experiment. Play. You can choose to read through the exercises now and implement them later.

SEE YA, TENSION

Tension ain't solidity, so let go of it. I used to carry so much tension in my shoulders. I think I was subconsciously pushing them upward and forward to make myself look bigger and more imposing. Why? Because deep down I felt small, but it only made me look tense and like I was uptight, guarded or even defeated… not bigger. Creating unnecessary tension in the body is not the same as solidity and will likely hinder your process of building it.

It's been debated whether or not the emotional and physical selves are actually interconnected. I believe they are. Let's take a look at the most common areas of the body where we tend to carry tension and how it can be linked to an internal or external cause. I'll include a few general ways to release the tension; however, if you find one of these areas is particularly problematic for you, a quick internet search will land you on several guided videos and articles with more detailed techniques. Even if you can only devote five minutes a day to releasing unwanted tension, you will absolutely notice an improvement. Please also be conscientious in ruling out illness and injury with a visit to the appropriate professional if necessary.

Shoulders & Neck. This is probably the number one problem area. Tension here is usually a result of too many stresses and responsibilities. It kind of gives meaning to the phrase "carrying the weight of the world on your shoulders." When we're overwhelmed from a chaotic personal or professional life, this is the primary area in which unreleased emotional stress tends to store itself. It can develop for a number of other reasons, including poor posture, how we sit during the day, how we sleep, or in my case, trying to make myself look bigger. There are tons of great stretches to release shoulder and neck tension. I found shoulder rolls helpful and easy to do any time of day, as well as consciously dropping my shoulders downward and backward throughout the day until it became second nature.

Face & Jaw. Tension held in the face often goes to the jaw and results in clenching or teeth-grinding. Sometimes the tension is held in the brow area, which can lead to headaches, hard frown lines, or regularly looking angry or confused. Some men do this intentionally, often for social media photos, because they feel a hardened facial expression denotes a hardened persona. Alas, it does not. It just looks silly and creates unnecessary tension. Sometimes tension can settle in this area as a result of physical or emotional stress. To release it, try contracting or stretching different facial muscles for 10 seconds and then fully relaxing them in reps of three to five. One mentor I worked with had her students make funny faces and hold them for a few seconds and release. It's a good stretch for the jaw, tongue, nose and brow – the whole face, really, if you're willing to get a little ugly.

Chest. When guys puff their chest out or walk around with it constantly flexed, it restricts movement in the upper body, it restricts the breath and they often appear guarded. Guarded is not synonymous with strong. Conscious or subconscious muscular tension in the chest is often a result of repressed emotional pain or emotionally protecting oneself. Releasing emotional pain is like releasing toxins. Get it out.

To address it physically, one of my favorite stretches is to simply lay on my back with my arms at 90-degree angles on both sides (think "surrender" position), making sure the backs of my hands are flat against the ground. For a more intense stretch, you can prop your chest up by putting a small pillow under your back.

Lungs & Diaphragm. This area can have some crossover with tension in the chest. The diaphragm holds all the stress and the lungs don't fully expand. I call it the "panic place." Tightness happens when we enter fight-or-flight mode, the breath stops at the chest and doesn't drop down to the bottom of the lungs. The anxiety is usually the result of suppressing something we don't want to deal with. Sadness, pain and rage can manifest this way when they have been contained for too long. The shortness of breath it causes puts us in panic mode and affects our rational thinking. It's not to be mistaken for healthy adrenaline which is rooted in readiness. This is rooted in fear. Some side stretches will open up the intercostal muscles that help facilitate breathing.

You can also stimulate the diaphragm. Place one hand on your stomach and the other on your chest. Try humming or making a vowel sound and see if you can create a resonance on the hand pressed against your stomach. Next, try breathing and pushing out that same hand with your breath. Do both of these exercises several times. The exercises for the chest, lungs and diaphragm work well together.

Lower Back. The lower back is the foundation of your back strength. Keeping it strong and tension-free is essential for an upright, solid posture. Tension in the lower back can be due to a number of reasons, ranging from sports related injuries to a slouchy posture. Guys who lift heavy weights often complain of tightness in the lower back, which can be a result of poor form or weak core muscles. Guys who sit at a desk all day may need to invest in an ergonomic office chair or get more exercise. It's said that guilt, shame, and a lack of self-worth are the emotions to explore when lower back tension is psychosomatic. Child's pose is an easy yoga pose and great for stretching out the lower back for some immediate relief of tension. Walking daily is a great way to maintain looseness in the lower back long-term.

Stomach. Yeah, we can carry tension here, too, and it sucks. It can be a result of indigestion, IBS, or in many cases, anxiety. When we're faced with a conflict or big decision, this seems to be the body's favorite place to malfunction as a way of letting us know there's something we need to accept or resolve. The best thing you can do to relieve some of that tension is to identify and acknowledge whatever it is you're grappling with, then talk about it with someone you trust and get it out. It might be scary and uncomfortable, but it will likely release the hold it has on your body. In other cases, the tightness is due to dietary issues and our gut is in need of a healthier lifestyle to reduce the tension over time. Consider a few sessions with a nutritionist.

Hips. Stiffness in the hips can affect your posture by making it difficult to stand up straight. It can make you feel the need to shift your weight to one hip, creating imbalance and taking away the power in your stance. Tension in the hips can stem from a multitude of issues, such as sitting for too long, leaning to one side when standing, sleeping on the same side all night, or even tightness in other parts of the body. The hips are another one of the body's "fight or flight" stress response areas. In yoga, hip opening stretches are often the ones responsible for releasing a flood of stored emotions, sometimes resulting in tears. The butterfly stretch is a good hip opener. Sit with your back straight and the soles of your feet pressed together in front of you. Your knees will bend to both sides. Try pulling your heels closer toward you, leaning forward with a straight back and pushing your knees downward to deepen the stretch in 20-second intervals.

GROUND THAT POSTURE

There's a reason why superheroes are almost always drawn with both feet planted firmly on the ground and their weight evenly balanced between them. It's the same reason four-legged animals will stand on their hind legs, making themselves taller when they want to intimidate an opponent. The primal association with a tall, erect posture is stability and power. Besides being important for our bone and muscle health, posture is also good for the psyche. I believe posture is indicative of what's going on inside our head, and, respectively, that what we feel can be precipitated by our posture. Those who stand grounded, centered, and erect might be feeling confident, authoritative, and courageous, and by positioning ourselves this way, we can possibly generate those same feelings. It happens for me every time I catch myself slipping and reground my posture. I *feel* different. You'll see!

Grounding your posture is about controlling your center of gravity and standing tall. Before we get into how to do those two things, it's worth mentioning that maintaining a healthy weight and a strong core are crucial for your posture. If you need to improve either or both of those areas, make a mental note and continue reading. Do not skip this section because you have physical health issues or a long weight-loss journey. There is still plenty you can do now.

Find your center of gravity. It is where you carry the bulk of your weight. A bowling ball has a center of gravity right in the middle of it, because the weight is evenly distributed throughout its sphere shape. We tend to carry more weight in the upper part of our body, so our center of gravity is not going to be perfectly centered. It is slightly above the waist area, about two inches below the navel. We lean to one side and our center of gravity has shifted, causing us to lose our balance or topple over if we're not careful.

Awareness of your center of gravity will naturally stabilize you, and consciously keeping it aligned with your head and spine is going to help solidify your posture. Try standing barefoot and focusing your attention on the bottoms of your feet. Let yourself feel the pressure of the ground beneath you against each foot. Balance your weight evenly between them by pointing your feet forward and positioning them shoulder-width apart. Unlock your knees and bounce a little, but leave your feet planted. Sway from side to side, shifting your center of gravity back and forth between each foot to feel the difference in weight. Then recenter the weight evenly again. Let your feet do all the work right now. Let go of your ass. Let go of your quads. Drop your shoulders - you don't need them. Your center of gravity is stabilized by your feet now.

To maximize your stability even more, let's make sure you're using your whole foot to support your weight. Try to visualize three points on the bottom of each foot like an imaginary tripod: one right below the big toe, one right below the pinky toe, and one right in the center of the heel. Imagine steel beams coming from each of those three points shooting 20 feet into the ground beneath you, anchoring each foot into place. Grip the ground with those three points to activate them, then balance your body weight evenly among them on each foot. Now you're centered and stable. Stay like that for a bit and embrace the new feeling. Try to let go of any unnecessary tension or stiffness in other parts of the body. You can actually relax into this position and still maintain a stable and confident appearance. Try having a conversation with someone in this position. Supporting your weight this new way may feel awkward at first and take a lot of your focus, but with practice it will become second nature and you'll be able to maintain it and remain present.

Stand tall. Standing upright with a straight spine is the second half of grounding yourself. It supports a healthy spine, saves you from back problems later in life and makes you look and feel taller. I like to use the wall-sit exercise to rebuild my spine whenever I feel myself beginning to slouch.

Start by standing with your heels about 12 inches from the wall behind you and lean your butt against the wall. Your knees should be bent at about a 45-degree angle. Remember to keep the energy in your feet; this is not meant to be a leg workout, though you may notice your quads and glutes wanting to engage. Now drop your upper body all the way forward as if to touch your toes. Maintaining your balance through your feet, try letting your arms and head hang like dead weight. Let them bounce and swing a little to ensure you've released your grip on them. Now you're going to use your core - a lot. Ever so slowly, start to roll yourself upward while continuing to keep the arms and head dead weight. Use the wall as your guide. The lowest vertebra of the spine should make contact with the wall first. Then the next. And the next. Keep each vertebra of the spine in contact with the wall behind you, and continue rolling upward using the strength of your core only. Take your time with this exercise! It should be strenuous and take several minutes. If you rush, you'll almost certainly lose contact with the wall. The idea is to stack and rebuild your spine vertebra by vertebra into a perfectly erect structure. With each incremental move upward, pause and take a breath, and give your spine a moment to settle into position, maintaining its contact with the wall at all times. It'll get tricky when you get to your neck because the back of your head won't allow those top vertebrae of the spine to touch the wall. Instead, focus on keeping the chin tucked in and looking straight ahead.

Once you're fully upright, take a few moments to embrace the connection between the wall and your spine. Relax into the position by releasing any unnecessary tension. When you feel ready, put all of the weight back on your two feet and walk around the room a bit. Do you feel more upright? Do you feel taller? What effect does it have on your mental or emotional state? Let it make you feel proud, confident, and strong.

Practice both exercises as often as you need to! Something you can do in between that's helped me big time in maintaining my posture is taking walks while wearing a weightlifting belt. They help lifters keep their back straight and their core engaged. For your purpose, you'll want one that's not leather and not too protrusive, so you can comfortably wear it under a shirt for an hour or so.

CLAIM YOUR SPACE

Business leaders, politicians, academic experts, and even FBI agents have noted that broader, more open postures change the perceptions of others and also of the individuals, themselves. Mentally and physically claiming your space exudes an energy that says "I belong here." Closed-in, compressed positioning says "I don't want to be here" or "I don't deserve to be here." If you find yourself inclined to take up as little space as possible, you may want to check in and ask yourself "Why am I hiding?"

A few summers ago, I met up with several friends and acquaintances for a long weekend of beach parties, bar hopping, dancing, and socializing. There were several people I was excited to hang out with, so this was something I was really looking forward to, despite not being a huge fan of the party scene. Massive crowds are not my idea of fun the way they used to be in my twenties. Nonetheless, after getting settled into my hotel, I couldn't wait to run right over to one of the most packed happy-hour events of all the bars on the stretch. I was literally radiating with excitement up until the moment I walked through the door and saw the crowd. That's when I felt a little social anxiety. I hadn't been in a crowd like that in years. It used to be my scene when I tended bar in some of the most well-known bars and clubs in New York City, but it wasn't anymore. I was out of my comfort zone and I felt it. This wasn't my world anymore and I felt like I didn't belong. Where the fuck am I and what is my old ass doing here? I hope no one talks to me. That's what I told myself. No one did. Absolutely no one talked to me. I made my way through the crowd until I found one of my friends. He looked at me and said, "Relax. Have a drink."

The next day, I decided to mentally prep myself prior to the big happy hour party. I started with a little meditation and some stretches. I told myself I belong. I told myself these were my people and I want to be seen. I deserve to be seen. I'm an important member of the party. That day, I didn't just walk in like I belonged. I walked in like I owned the fucking place. "Hey, everyone, welcome to my party. I hope you're all having a great time." That's what went through my head as I walked through the crowd. I must have been approached by 10 or 15 people, some strangers, before I got to my friends. I wasn't wailing my arms around. I wasn't naked. I wasn't dressed up like a giraffe. I wasn't gratuitously demanding attention in any way. Nope. It was not about that. It was about ownership and openness. Let's take a look at how the body expresses those two things.

Own your space. Ownership of the space you're in is achieved internally, but manifests externally. We all have our personal space and we know that it belongs to us. We generally do not like having it violated unless we have verbally or non-verbally invited someone into it. Beyond your personal space is your space in the room or surroundings you're a part of. We can own that, too. The first step is to be present. Do that by answering these questions:

Where am I? Look around and acknowledge the room, atmosphere, event, and how far that space expands.

Who am I? Identify the person or people who are also a part of that space and your relationship to them.

Why am I here? This is not a challenge, but an affirmation that you belong in this space. Find reasons that you deserve to be here as much as everyone else who's a part of the space with you.

You won't be able to do this while you're looking at your phone or daydreaming. It forces you to be present and to take in your surroundings. Keep your head up and start acknowledging the things and people around you. Make eye contact with whomever you want. They'll notice you back. Imagine your space expanding outward as you become a part of the space you're in. You're bigger than just your personal space. You're an important part of this larger space and you deserve to be here. Own that space and feel good about it being yours and it will change you physically.

Stay open and available. Openness is about having a physical demeanor that says you are confident and available. An open posture communicates interest, readiness, and comfort. The more open you are, the more space you appear to take up, the larger your presence. If you often struggle to convince yourself that you belong, you can learn to turn your focus to your exterior. It won't matter what you're feeling inside if the exterior says, "I'm open and available." People believe what your body tells them.

An open posture is one that is grounded and facing your audience, whether that be one person or a room full of people. Face your feet and your body in their direction. Keep your torso unblocked by leaving your hands at your sides and in view. If you're seated, your hands can rest on your legs or you can take advantage of the armrests if available, opening up your posture even more. Folding your hands in front of you, putting them in your pockets or crossing your arms reads as submissive or guarded. We often do this subconsciously when we're uncomfortable or feeling defensive. In some instances, deliberately folded arms can read as authoritative, but even then it closes us off. Be specific and use them appropriately or not at all.

The same applies to our legs. Keep them open to the width of your shoulders when seated or standing. Opening them too wide when standing might take up more space, but it also shortens you. Opening them too wide when seated can appear too informal or like you're trying too hard to look relaxed. Of course, I'm not saying you should not spread your legs comfortably when you're at home with a friend. Use your judgment based on the setting and relationship with the person in front of you; and when in doubt, revert to shoulder width. Create a habit of keeping both feet firmly planted on the ground. Crossed legs appear slightly less assertive and less engaged. In certain instances, such as when seated in a casual social setting, deliberately crossed legs can say "I'm relaxed and comfortable with you." Sure, that can be a very good thing, but there are plenty of other ways to communicate that. Practicing keeping both feet on the ground is a good starting point when learning openness.

These positions might feel awkward initially. You may think you look stiff and self-conscious, and struggle to figure out what the hell to do with your hands. Don't worry! You'll get the hang of it. That's why it's important to practice these positions and relaxing into them as often as possible. Do them alone first. Next, try them when you're on the phone with someone or when in the company of a person you are comfortable with. Eventually try them in public. They will become second nature over time.

WATCH THEM GESTURES, SON

This part is a lot of fun because we get to be super specific in refining the details of how we communicate physically. Are you ready to get into a little kinesics science? Kinesics is the study of the way in which certain body movements and gestures serve as a form of nonverbal communication. There are five categories of kinesics: emblems, illustrators, affective displays, regulators, and adaptors. We're going to focus on illustrators.

Illustrators are physical movements that complement our verbal communication by describing, accenting, or reinforcing what we're saying as we speak. We use illustrators to indicate the size of an object or to draw a picture in the air or to emphasize a key word. Pointing to an object in the room and pounding on the table are both ways to illustrate. The frequency may vary by culture, but they are used widely. Use of illustrators can help indicate interest, emphasis, and also enthusiasm for the topic being discussed.

Illustrators are also the most common type of gesture and, because they tend to happen subconsciously and frequently as we speak, they're an accurate showcase of our physical mannerisms. Physical mannerisms show up in plenty of situations other than in illustrators, such as when we eat, the way we hold our phones, nervous tics, and so on. However, for most of us, they show up most abundantly when we communicate. Honing our illustrator habits will most likely translate over time to the other areas.

Take a second to think about men's mannerisms. Can you think of a man whose mannerisms you like? It can be someone in your life or someone in the media. Once you have someone in mind, picture the way they use their hands as they speak. What do you notice? It might be difficult to pin down the specifics, but see if they align with any of my findings below. After some research, I found the most keen and objective observers of stereotypical masculine mannerisms were made by women transitioning to men or female-to-male sex reassignment. I read several forums and these three characteristics were repeated the most when it came to men's illustrators. See if there's anything in these observations that aligns with the style you want.

Men move slower. The observation here was that men, in general, are less expressive and therefore tend to have slower physical gestures when they communicate. That said, I don't believe that less expression always means a more manly man. As an Italian-American man, I can attest that there are plenty of very expressive men who are admired by other men. Take Al Pacino, for example. For many men, he epitomizes masculinity, and Tony Montana was anything but unexpressive. Let's frame this observation differently. What if slowing down doesn't have to mean less expressive, but rather more deliberate? One of the first principles of strong speech taught in public speaking is to take your time. Speaking too fast deprives your voice of rhythm, good resonance, and, ultimately, the attention of your listeners. Slower, more deliberate speech commands the attention of your audience. Slowing your illustrators and making them more deliberate can punctuate your words and make them more powerful. One way to start practicing this is to imagine your hands are moving underwater as you illustrate.

No limp wrists. In ancient Rome, rhetoric teachers discouraged a limp wrist when speaking to the public. It was thought of along the same lines as a slouched posture - while it might feel more comfortable to slouch or let one's wrist be relaxed and unengaged, it was deemed as lazy or having a lack of control over the body. Posture and mannerisms were a portrayal of character, and a solid wrist meant a solid man. Today, some groups and social circles have adopted the limp wrist as part of their individuality. There's nothing right or wrong about it, but I think it makes sense to understand how your society defines it and if it aligns with the style you want for yourself.

One way to avoid a limp wrist is to consciously keep your wrists engaged. Lead with the hand rather than the forearm and your illustrators go from fluid to solid. Imagine waving a flag. The pole (your forearm) is stable and the fabric (the wrist, hands and fingers) is limp. The pole dictates all movement of the fabric. The weight of the flag is all in the pole, so when the pole moves, the fabric follows behind it, gliding and dancing through the air. Now imagine swinging an axe. The weight of the axe is not in the handle, but at the head of the axe. The head of the axe leads all of the movement. It cuts through the air and the handle follows. The weight distribution is the opposite of a flag. If you were to apply the axe metaphor to your movements, the wrists will always be engaged and you'll lead with your hands. You'll swing an axe rather than wave a flag.

Less is more. Less expression means less movement means more manly. Eh, I say bullshit. But less movement does force us to find other ways to be expressive, such as facial expressions, the words we say, and the way we say them. I remember several times when being filmed in a tight shot, all of my emoting had to be done with my face and voice because my arms were completely out of frame. You might think an easy solution would be to use your hands since they're off-camera and then everything caught in-frame will appear organic. Not exactly. Moving your arms off-camera can create movement in the shoulders, neck, and head, which can be jarring for the watcher. Even eyebrows jumping up and down are a no-no for a super tight shot. Imagine being in the movie theater and the face on screen is 12 feet wide. Bouncing eyebrows would be incredibly distracting. The person being filmed needs to remain still in these cases and everything they express needs to come through their eyes and their voice. It's a good exercise, and not just for an actor. It teaches us how much we rely on our hands to express ourselves.

You can do this at home by imagining you're framed from your chest up, arms completely off-camera. Now try talking about something that excites you. Be descriptive and use details to explain something specific. See how often you feel the urge to use your hands. If the imaginary frame doesn't work, try sitting on your hands.

LEAD WITH YOUR LEFT

They say when marching at arms, the weapon is carried on the right and when getting ready to attack, the left foot leads.

Why should you lead with your left when walking? Because it will give your walk a natural rhythm, though you can do the exact same thing by leading with your right. The point is to lead with one. Take note how it affects the cadence of your walk. Here's a few more tips to a solid, confident walk.

Take longer strides. It shows confidence in where you are going. Small steps are usually taken when we are apprehensive. Lengthen your steps to what feels comfortable to your leg length. Like everything else discussed in this chapter, start big and gradually lessen it to what feels comfortable.

Walk with some pep. Walking with purpose means you have a destination. It means you have somewhere to be because you're important. See what it feels like if you start walking a little faster. You can always adjust it based on circumstance.

Make eye contact. Acknowledge the passerby. It shows self assurance. Looking down or avoiding eye contact can read as discomfort, fear or disinterest. Be engaged with your surroundings and notice who you're passing. Based on where you are in the world, the social convention for how long is appropriate to maintain eye contact with a stranger varies. To start, try one second or the time it takes to say hello in your head, then move your focus back to your destination straight ahead. Feel free to add a nod of acknowledgement. This seems to be pretty universally accepted.

Implement everything else in this chapter. It all applies to walking. Be mindful to rid yourself of any unnecessary tension or stiffness as you walk. Maintain an upright posture with the shoulders back, accentuating the chest. Claim your space by keeping the feet shoulder-width apart. You can opt for wider if it feels organic and comfortable, but be aware that going narrower will create a sway in your hips you may not want. You can stay open by keeping your hands out of your pockets, and stay present by keeping your head held up. An occasional glance at the ground to see where you're stepping is fine, but don't put your focus there. Head up says "I'm confident and feeling good."

PHYSICAL STRENGTH DOES MATTER

Guys, we need to acknowledge that men with a strong, muscular physique are often regarded as more powerful, authoritative, and masculine. While it pains me deeply to see a man completely neglect the inner self and all other virtues of masculinity, putting all of his focus into getting jacked so he can impress other men with his biceps, we simply cannot deny the effect a man's physique has on most of us. It may be archaic thinking, but if I put my life on it, it won't change. I believe it is a primitive, inherent part of our programming that will never be completely resolved, and despite the persistent efforts of pop psychology and modern marketing, size does matter… to *some* degree.

I'm 5′ 9″ which is right around average height for a man, however my skeletal frame is not very wide. Prior to building muscle, I appeared small in stature and a bit frail. It was not the look I wanted and it certainly did not match my personality. Sure, I could still be a bold and courageous leader, but if men looked at me and thought "I could knock his ass to the ground with ease," how much did they actually respect me? Over the course of my 20s, I went from 130lbs to 200lbs. My body fat percentage increased as well, but most of the gains were muscle.
Shortly after the last 20lbs of gains, I remember being on vacation in Cancun at a very busy resort. Without consciously changing anything about my behavior, I was taken aback by how many men *noticed* me. I was getting bro-greetings of acknowledgment left and right. Some were verbal, some simply a nod, some in passing, and some even at the urinal. Some of the patrons and staff even found reasons to start a conversation with me. A few referenced weight-lifting, such as asking what supplements I use

or how often I train. The level of respect I got without changing any of my behaviors was fascinating. I almost felt like I was walking around in a different body. Well, I was. It was still my body, but it wasn't the same body I had spent the majority of my life in. It was my new body with the same me inside operating it, but men regarded me differently now.

Physical strength *does* matter.

Besides the impact it has on the respect we get from the outside world, building physical strength supports physical and mental health, it teaches us resilience and discipline, it underscores our other virtues, it makes us more capable and confident, and it is an essential part of crafting ourselves as men. You can decide how far you want to go with strength training and exercise. It can be something you work at for a few hours a week or it can be one of your greatest passions. If you've read this far, then you already know that I don't think the gym should be the only place and time you feel confident as a man. Yes, I'm talking to you. Balance is key. Balance it with your other goals. I do, however, think it's important that some form of strength training becomes a part of your lifestyle in one way or another.

Sometimes nature works against us, but that doesn't mean it's our destiny. We do what we can with what we've been given. We can learn to accept our limitations as part of loving ourselves, while simultaneously working to reach the full potential of what nature has given us. There are guys out there doing fucking pull-ups in wheelchairs. No excuses.

"Sickly, an uncoordinated weakling with the pale fragile hands of a girl, speaking with a lisp and a slight stutter, he had been at the mercy of bullies. They beat him, ridiculed him, and pelted him with cricket balls. Trembling and humiliated, he hid in a nearby woods. This was

hardly the stuff of which gladiators are made. His only weapons were an unconquerable will and an incipient sense of immortality...

Beginning at the age of seven, Churchill deliberately set out to change his nature, to prove that biology need not be destiny. His head was ponderous, his limbs small, his belly tumescent, his chest puny. His skin was so sensitive that he broke into a rash unless he slept naked at night between silk sheets. By day he could wear only silk underwear against his skin. Endomorphs are characteristically lazy, calculating, easygoing, and predictable. Churchill was none of these. He altered his emotional constitution to that of an athlete, projecting the image of a valiant, indomitable bulldog.

At times along the way, he despaired. In 1893, he wrote, 'I am cursed with so feeble a body, that I can hardly support the fatigues of the day.' Yet he was determined to prove just as hardy as any mesomorph. In his teens he nearly killed himself while leaping from a bridge during a game of tag; he pitched down almost 30 feet and lay unconscious for three days. He fell again steeplechasing at Aldershot, and yet again when disembarking at Bombay, where he permanently injured a shoulder; for the rest of his active life he played polo, off and on, with his arm bound to his side. As a child he caught pneumonia. He suffered from chest ailments the rest of his life. He was allergic to anesthetics and periodically erupted in boils. Nevertheless, he refused to yield to human frailty. In his inner world there was no room for concessions to weakness. He never complained of fatigue. In his 70th year he flew to councils of war overseas sprawled across a tick mattress on the floor of an unheated World War II bomber...He will be remembered as freedom's champion in its darkest hour, but he will be cherished as a man."

Manchester, W. (1984). The Last Lion:
Winston Spencer Churchill: Visions of Glory, 1874-1932.
Bantam; Reissue Edition

Each of these sections can be treated like a prerequisite to the next, so try to assess them in the order I've written them. Think about grading yourself before you move on to the next section. You need a C to pass, and you can always go back later and bump that up to a B. For now, pay closest attention to the sections you feel need the most improvement.

When it comes to making significant changes to your physical behavior, you'll want to focus on one area at a time. The goal is to make the adjustments second nature. That means you could pour a cup of coffee while having a difficult conversation and still maintain those adjustments to your posture on which you've been working. In order to get there, it will have to live in your conscious mind for a while. Days. Weeks. Maybe months. It depends on how big of an adjustment you want to make and how much time you devote to practicing it. The body might fight you in the beginning - the new information you give it may conflict with what it's used to. Fight back by practicing. Repetition is key. The body eventually accepts. You'll be amazed when it does. If you need a little inspiration, go check out the film, *My Left Foot*. You will need to constantly remind yourself that Daniel Day Lewis does not actually have cerebral palsy. Through diligent practice, he trained his body to take on the physical behaviors of someone with CP. He did this while simultaneously reciting lines he memorized and staying emotionally connected to the circumstances of each scene. I'm not asking the same of you. You do not need to be an Oscar-worthy actor to pull this off. But you do need diligence and patience. There is nothing mystical about this process. It is purely technical. Practice until the body accepts.

NOTES

NOTES

CRAFTING

MASCULINITY

Ch6: Aligning Principles

(nobility)

Is nobility an important part of crafting masculinity?

The men I have admired most and who have had the greatest impact on my life have all had noble hearts. Noble leaders have taught me magnanimity and benevolence, my greatest mentors exemplified nobility through humility and compassion, and my most noble friends have shown me the value of loyalty and bravery – all qualities I strive for and all qualities I see men admiring in other men.

So how does one achieve nobility? Easy: by having and adhering to a set of principles that inform high moral action and good character. Seems straightforward enough, right? We all have principles we've learned throughout life. Let's recap the ones you were taught in childhood…

Be kind to others.
Always tell the truth.
Never cheat.
Share with others.

Any of them ring a bell? We probably learned even more through adolescence and different stages of adulthood…

Always be on time.
Keep your commitments.
Never exploit others.
Always give your best effort.

Are you keeping up? Great. So could you recite all of these principles to me right now then? Are you consciously practicing them with diligence?

Having too many principles can be counterproductive. We can lose track of them all and, in an effort to simplify them, blur them into one general principle to *be a good person*. That's a bit too subjective to apply to all life circumstances, and too general to understand the specific virtues that make up your nobility. On the other hand, if we don't have enough principles, we could often end up feeling conflicted on *how* to navigate to high moral action. Here's something else to consider: are your principles rules or guidelines? What I mean is are they universal absolutes that can only be interpreted one way and require a strict adherence? Or is there some flexibility based on your own personal values and the circumstance? Some of the guys I've worked with have complained that adhering to their principles like they're carved in stone has actually produced more conflict in their life than it has nobility. Others have said that using them too loosely has led to them making immoral choices because it suited a selfish need or desired outcome rather than noble action. Suddenly, nobility doesn't seem so straightforward anymore, huh?

Whether or not nobility is an important part of becoming the man you want to be is totally up to you. The ongoing debate of principles and whether or not we even need them will likely take its rightful place as one of moral philosophy's greatest battles. Personally, I can't ignore that nobility has been a common virtue of heroic men (fictional and non-fictional) throughout history. Principles are my navigation system to nobility. I moderate my adherence to them, and that's why they've served me well so far; definitely not because I found the perfect ones. It's ultimately going to be up to you to decide which principles you use and how you adhere to them.

In this chapter, I want to help you organize your principles and understand the purpose they serve. I'm also going to challenge your principles for the sake of ironing out any subjectivity and hopefully providing you with a more direct route to the reason you're using them. I'm going to objectively share with you everything I've learned about principles in my personal and professional life, especially specific to men. I believe they can be incredibly useful when they are aligned with our personal values. Alignment is key. To find that alignment, we need to reassess the principles you're using and see that each one truly serves and supports your journey to being the man you want to be.

WHY PRINCIPLES ARE IMPORTANT

First, let's break down some of the reasons why having principles is important. I'm also going to point out some of the differences between principles and personal values here, since they're often used interchangeably but are not the same.

Principles give us structure. Humans generally do well with structure and order - something we're taught from early childhood. In school, we have structure. At home, we have structure. In religion, we have structure. In society, in the military, at work, at the bar, on social media, at the pool, in the gym, we have structure. For most, there's an inclination to adhere to it and even to enforce it. Generally speaking, when we give something structure, we have order. Principles make this fairly easy by spelling it out for us: *Always do this...* or *Never do this...* While we may not always like them, they are usually easy to abide by. Ex: *Always treat others how you want to be treated.*

Principles are easy to understand. Principles are essentially distillations of complex ideology or generalizations of millions of cases reduced into one universal sentence. While a diligent assessment and implementation of our values might be sufficient for living a life that feels rich with purpose, values are personal and, therefore, a lot more open to interpretation than principles. Our values are simplified into four words that hold a ton of personal meaning underneath them. *Strength* can refer to physical power to one person, while it can signify perseverance and courage to another. There are layers and layers of personal meaning below the surface of each value. Over time, we may forget some of that meaning, and then it reverts to a more general meaning that we're no longer able to live and act by purposefully. Principles, on the other hand, are usually clear and concise sentences with a meaning that remains stable and unchanging. Ex: *Keep your commitments.*

Principles make the world better. At least, that's the intention. Principles are usually about serving the greater good of humanity by doing what's right - an area I once struggled with because I used to question whether right and wrong exist, but we'll get into that later. Principles discern right and wrong for us and often imply that everyone should live by them. They acknowledge that we are a part of something much bigger than ourselves and that our actions have an impact on the overall integrity of that thing - that thing being mankind. Some values only serve us and our own selfish needs and wants. Principles, on the other hand, are thousands of years of human experience distilled down to a simple, but straightforward moral code of how to be a good human. In this regard, they hold us personally accountable and give us something to stand for.

They're also great for children since they have not fully developed their humanity or empathy and don't yet know their values. Teaching them principles often has a great influence on their values as adults. Ex: *Always tell the truth.*

MORAL PARTICULARISM FOR $1000

Now, let's take a look at principles through a different lens; one that highlights problems with a strict adherence to anything that might be considered morally universal or generalized. For instance, what would you do in a situation where two of your principles are in conflict with one another? Let's say one of your principles is never to hit a woman and another one of your principles is to always protect your family. What would you do if you were witnessing your elderly mother being beaten unconscious by three homeless women who were trying to rob her? There's no one else in sight, so you can't yell for help. You can call the police, but by the time they arrive, your mother will be dead. You can try restraining one of the women, but you can't hold back all three. You are, however, strong enough to stop all of them, but it's going to take a few mighty blows. Remember, though, your principle says you can never hit a woman. Your other principle says you always protect your family. Now what? You had this perfect moral system working for you all your life… this set of rules that tell you exactly what is morally right in any possible case. All you have to do is follow them… right? Wrong. In this case, one must be broken and there is no way around it. So, what can you do? The proposed argument to consider is that all principles have exceptions and cannot possibly apply to all life circumstances.

(Enter moral particularism)

Moral particularism started trending in the last 10 years. It's gaining traction in philosophical circles as it challenges thousands of years of moral philosophy. The claim is that moral principles are neither necessary nor sufficient for guiding us to moral action. Particularists also believe that the application of general moral principles inhibits proper moral judgment because we rely on the precision of the principle to guide our actions rather than ourselves. Relying on a generalized principle that, according to particularists, cannot possibly be applied to all cases that present similar features that correspond with the principle, could lead us to go against our natural inclinations and make poor choices. Moral philosophy posits that the precipitating feature in one case will hold the very same precipitating nature and have the same impact on any other case. Moral particularism proposes that a precipitating feature in one case may have a different impact altogether or no impact at all on another case.

Particularist philosophy isn't new. Some theorists suggest it dates as far back as BC, and that Aristotle may have been the original gangster who challenged moral generalizations and suggested that aiming for exactness is faulty. Where do you stand? Does it make you question the validity or sufficiency of your own principles? See where it takes you.

IT'S THE PRINCIPLE... OR MY PRIDE?

We can't talk principles and not talk pride. It's another area of much-needed examination as the two so often get confused. They couldn't be more different in meaning, yet the actions and behaviors driven by them can look similar. We can sometimes convince ourselves we're acting on principle when actually it's pride that has a hold on us. Additionally, the common accusation that men are too principled is often coupled with the accusation that men are too prideful.

Does this mean principles and pride go hand in hand? Hell no. Pride is self-serving and will completely shit on your principles. To figure out where the crossover is happening, let's start by answering the frequently asked question, "Why are men so principled?" Principles are essentially ideals and men can be very idealistic and rational, sometimes to a fault. The proposition of being the ideal man and living the ideal life by following a set of idealistic principles might seem totally logical and rational in concept. This + this = this, right? It's a very practical perspective, albeit limited, that makes everything black and white and easy to understand. It suggests a world that has no grays, no blurs or curves; only hard facts, tangible things and perfect, geometric shapes. In that world, a set of hard rules can be applied and the promise of perfection by a strict adherence to them can be made. A lot of men think this way for a few reasons. First, it's easy to follow rules once we know and understand them. Second, it removes the fear of the unknown. Third, it ultimately puts us in control of everything.

As incomplete and erroneous as this thinking may seem, it *doesn't* guarantee you *won't* be successful. While it may prove to be problematic in certain areas of their life, such as interpersonal relationships, it certainly can hold up in some industries and positions. Men who think this way might do well as software engineers, accountants, investment bankers, chemists, and more. Unfortunately, this kind of idealistic, black-and-white thinking can devolve over time to the "I'm right, you're wrong" mentality, which is no longer on course with serving universal morals. It produces an inflated ego and a false sense of superiority over others. The principles get lost and the satisfaction in one's own abilities takes over, giving pride the opportunity to drive moral action.

Another reason many men might seem overly principled is because of the desire for honor. A lot of men want to be deemed honorable by other men, respected for their achievements and for having high moral worth. When a man exhibits notable courage or loyalty, risking or sacrificing his life for his country, he is usually honored. When a man exhibits notable strength or excellence, making an outstanding achievement in his work, he is usually honored. Similarly, when a man exhibits notable temperance, humanity and wisdom through an impeccable adherence to moral code, he is also usually honored. Most of the men I've worked with and know personally want to be honored.

However, if a man lets his desire for honor drive him more than honor itself, his actions may be fueled by a self-fulfilled moral superiority: pride.

Now that we see where some crossover might be happening, and how principles and pride can get blurred, I'm going to share a little story with you that I think nicely portrays two men acting on pride.

I was at the grocery store with a buddy of mine I was visiting for the weekend, accompanying him as he picked up a few things he needed. We were both a little hungover from the night before, but otherwise in good spirits and anticipating the next round of partying and club-hopping that would ensue that evening. We were in our twenties – remember when you could party two or three nights in a row like it was nothing?

As we were checking out, I observed an odd transaction that, at the time, I didn't fully understand. As the cashier scanned a bag of chips and proceeded to bag them, my friend stopped her. "Wait. Those were marked as a dollar."

The cashier paused. They had rung up as $2.49. She glanced at her screen, then looked back over to my friend and responded. "They're a dollar when you buy three or more."

"They were marked as a dollar," my friend repeated.

"No," she replied, visibly somewhat annoyed by my friend's insistence, "they're marked as a dollar when you buy three or more. It says it underneath the price."

"Take them out of the bag. I don't want them." He did not skip a beat or show an ounce of emotion. I don't think he even made eye contact.

Okay, I get it. The tag was misleading. That's annoying. But, at the end of the day, my friend put the chips in the cart because he really wanted them, and I wanted him to have his chips.

"I'll pay for them," I chimed in. The cashier paused again, awaiting a verdict. Do the chips stay in the bag or come out of the bag? There's a line of people behind us waiting to checkout and go about their day.

"No, I don't want them," he replied, almost deadpan.

The fuck? This is getting silly. Smiling, and being maybe overly rational, I looked at my friend and said, "But, you *do* want them."

Maintaining the same poised and unaffected poker face, he muttered back, "It's the principle."

And that was that. The cashier set the bag of chips aside, rang up the rest of his items and we left.

So, what's the principle he was adhering to in that moment?

Never succumb to manipulative advertisements... even at the cost of denying yourself something you really want... over a dollar. Or maybe… *Always stand your ground... even in spite of yourself.*

The story continues. I went back and bought those fucking chips the very next day. I knew he wanted the stupid things and his decision to spite himself made no logical sense to me. Another part of it was my curiosity. How far was he willing to go to stand his ground and adhere to this supposed principle of his? Well, he denied the chips when I offered them to him the next day. He told me to keep them.

I didn't eat the chips... on principle, of course.

There is no exact method for extracting pride from principles or moral action. We need to remain aware of ourselves, and the next time we catch ourselves saying, "It's the principle," we should ask ourselves later, "Was it really?"

IDENTIFY YOUR PRINCIPLES

Someone for whom I have a lot of respect once told me that one should have no more than seven principles. He applied this to all models and believes that anymore than seven parts/aspects becomes difficult to remember. I concur, but use your best judgment. Start by getting your principles on paper or typed up in from of you. Think about the ones you learned in grade school, the ones you were taught by your parents and mentors, the ones you learned in your personal and professional adult life, any spiritual or religious ones and don't forget the ones you taught yourself.

If you feel like you have too many, eliminate any that you feel are no longer important to you or that you feel have become second nature. Consider combining ones that feel synonymous or similar. Leave the ones that mean the most to you today or that you want to work on the most. If you feel you don't have enough, use your top four (or top 10) values to come up with a list of seven or fewer sentences that turn each value into a personal principle. For example, if *Happiness* is one of your top values, you might say *Always do what makes you happy.* You can also use the list below as a reference. After taking an online poll of thousands of guys I asked to name an important principle they live by, these are the ones that were repeated the most:

Always be kind to others
Never give up
Accept what you can't control

Treat people fairly
Be honest with yourself and others
Try to see the good in everything
Stay open to change
Live in the moment
Stay true to yourself
Setting boundaries is okay
Let go of expectation
Always tell the truth
Give your best effort always
Never back down
Always put family first
Treat others how you want to be treated
Value process over outcome
Take responsibility for your actions
Respect yourself and others
Practice humility
Don't judge others
Be tolerant of differences
Never cheat
Be courageous always
Practice patience

FINALLY, ALIGNMENT

Next, we're going to take each principle through a scrutinizing series of questions for you to deliberate and ponder, leading up to the important decision of whether or not the principle can and should be revised. That's not cheating! I'm not suggesting you rewrite the Ten Commandments. I only want to broaden your perspective so that you can see that something like *Honor thy Father and thy Mother* is actually kinda subjective, and therefore you are left with the responsibility (or privilege, however you see it) of interpreting specifically what that means and looks like to you. My intention is for you to eventually have clarity and a set of principles that will help you achieve a feeling of nobility but also align with your personal values as often as possible. One by one, process each principle through this next set of questions. For each question, I've included an example.

Is there subjectivity? *Always do what's right.* Let's carefully consider the overwhelming subjectivity of *right*. Who decides what's *right*? You? Your parents? Pastor Darnell? The Quran? The Church of the Flying Spaghetti Monster? Who? Consider all words in your principle - look up each one's meaning if you must - make a note of any subjectivity and ask yourself what it means.

What does it mean to do right according to me?
What is the basis for these thoughts of right and wrong?

Are there exceptions? *Give your best effort always.* Hmmm... is there ever going to be a time in life when you are juggling multiple projects, all of great importance, and simply cannot spread yourself thin enough to give each one your best effort? For example, you have a work presentation to prepare, a project for a high-caliber client to complete, and a birthday party for your best friend to plan all by Friday. It's Monday. You've assessed the workload and know there is no way that all three can get 100% of your best effort without getting yourself sick from sleep deprivation. What do you do? One of them can only get 70% effort in order to knock the other two out of the park. Either that, or all three can get 90% but then none of them will be amazing.

One interpretation could be that this is an exception to the principle if you cannot postpone one of these three things. That would allow you to assess and prioritize in order to delegate your efforts the most efficiently. Another interpretation might be that even though one of these might get significantly less attention than the other two, you still will have given your best effort collectively to the three. Both interpretations hold up as truthful in my book, but it's something to consider for later. I believe a principle such as this one serves to make us noble by not slacking, therefore it's important to be certain that in cases similar to the example, the principle still serves its purpose. If too strict an adherence lands you in the hospital for a week because you gave 100% effort to all three things when you knew you couldn't, well, the principle didn't really serve its purpose, did it? Now you've lost a week of work and compromised your health. Make a note of any potential exceptions you foresee for your principle.

Does this align with my values? *Always put your family first.* This could be a religious principle, cultural principle, or one specific to your own family that's been instilled and passed down over generations. Let's say that you are a father and a husband. This principle suggests that you always put your spouse and kids before your job, and perhaps that seems morally sound to you.

Let's say, however, you're not a father or a husband. You have a very distant relationship with your siblings, but still speak to your mother regularly by phone. She's insisting you come visit for Easter weekend, but you just booked the biggest gig of your entire career and it requires you to work all through the weekend. Let's add on to this circumstance that your greatest value is growth. Booking this gig epitomizes growth to you and Mom just doesn't understand that. "Work is work and you should be with your family on the holidays." She's really laying the guilt on heavy. If you go home for Easter, you'll undoubtedly lose this opportunity and there's no guarantee that door will open again. On the other hand, not going home for Easter will upset Mom, but you can easily visit her the following weekend to make up for it. Does the family-first principle align with your values here? Note any conflicts with your principles and values.

Does this serve humanity or just me? *Always do what makes you happy.* Well, that will certainly align with a value of happiness, but will it make you a more noble man? Will it serve humanity? Perhaps being a happier man will make the world a better place. That's a good argument, but will this principle lead you to high moral action when you have to make a decision or is it too self-serving? These are the things I want you to think about with every principle. You certainly don't need to toss a principle simply because it serves your personal wellness and nothing more. However, if you are aiming for nobility, try to make sure you have enough principles that serve mankind and others more directly. Make a note of what and who each principle serves.

Remove, replace, rewrite, or reinterpret. This is where you make the call as to whether or not the principle is changeable or negotiable. I mean, according to many, if a principle is changeable, it becomes a guideline and is no longer a principle by definition. Oh well. The principle police aren't going to lock you up if you personalize your principle in a way that strays from alliance with its universal origin. Bottom line: they need to serve you and still align with your values. You make the call.

Can your principle be rewritten more specifically to resolve the subjectivity? *Always do what's right* might become *Do what you believe is right as often as you can.*

Can it be rewritten or replaced with another principle that will likely have less exceptions? *Give your best effort to everything you do* might be swapped with *Prioritize your duties so you can give 100% to the things that matter most.*

Can it be reinterpreted or removed altogether because it simply doesn't align with your values and beliefs today? *Always put your family first.* Maybe that doesn't work for you as a principle, despite your family virtues, so you'll remove it. Or maybe you can make it less absolute by interpreting it as *Family is a priority.*

Can it be rewritten, replaced, reinterpreted, or removed to better serve humanity and your goal of nobility? *Always do what makes you happy.* If you decide that you have enough principles that serve humanity or if nobility is not important to you, perhaps you'll decide this one needs to remain as is, absolute, and unchangeable. You may also determine that right now your mental health and wellness needs a little sprucing up, so you will keep it and swap it out in a later assessment.

I don't know about you, but I have certainly had fun challenging the shit out of your principles in this chapter. Hey look, if being a noble man is a virtue of yours and you use principles to keep you on that path, it's important to know where they come from and whether or not they're truly serving you. I know. It's a brain-workout of a process. Here's a virtual fist bump for your work.

Remember... understanding the loopholes or subjectivity of your principles can help you adjust them or your interpretation of them to better guide you to moral action. Discerning the difference between principles and pride will keep you striving for nobility and honor, rather than serving the ego. Processing your principles through the system of questions in this chapter will reinforce their meaning to you and ensure they are in alignment with your personal values. Lastly, be sure to put them somewhere that you will be able to see them easily.

NOTES

NOTES

(conviction)

CRAFTING

MASCULINITY

Ch7: Emboldening the Voice

What is a masculine voice?

The first, most obvious characteristic of a man's voice is a lower pitch range. Barry White spoke around the 71 Hz mark and Darth Vader spoke at about the 85 Hz mark. These are not attainable for most men. Let alone the probability that your voice will have very little musicality or variation at such a low pitch, you're probably not going to pull it off without forcing your larynx down and ultimately hurting yourself. The reality is that many men speak in a range that overlaps with the average range of women, and that's okay. What's more important is that you're using your full range.

So, what else makes a voice masculine? Looking at the speech patterns of men and women, here are some of the differences I've noticed besides pitch:

- Women tend to make more pitch changes when speaking, while men tend to use their range conservatively.
- Women tend to be more breathy as compared to men.
- Women tend to use their articulators more than men. Sometimes voice coaches describe this as "increased energy" around the articulators, especially the lips.

Does this mean that speaking in a tight-lipped, monotone Darth Vader voice is what you need to do to achieve a masculine voice? Hell no. Instead of trying to achieve a masculine voice, let's shift the focus to crafting your voice into one that is powerful, confident, and commands being heard - all qualities I think many of us respect in other men and all attainable.

First step is to start liking your voice. Scratch that, you don't have to like it yet, because we're going to enhance it. You have to *accept* it. You have a unique voice, unlike anyone else's. You have a voice that deserves to be heard. Owning it and embracing it is an act of authenticity and courage. It may seem backwards to accept your voice prior to refining it, but in order to craft your voice, you need to be starting from an authentic place. For example, if you have developed a habit of gripping the back of your throat to deepen your voice, we want to try to remove that first before we add the good stuff. A blank canvas is what we want. Try speaking with no effort regardless how much you dislike your natural speaking voice. Speak slowly, without thinking too much about it. Say out loud a few times:

"This is my natural voice. It's unique and not like anyone else's. I accept it and I own it. I commit to working on it, discovering what it can do and learning to love it. I deserve to be heard."

I love my voice today, but man, I didn't always. I hated it for a lot of my life. I remember cringing whenever I'd hear a recording of my voice. I'd be thinking "*That's* me?" I used to speak in my upper register a lot and often with an upward inflection, so whenever I'd hear myself, I thought I sounded like a girl. Not surprising that my speaking patterns were effeminate when most of my closest family members were females. I had two older sisters for role models, so I picked up a lot of their mannerisms growing up. When I got into my 20s, self-image became really important to me and I started to consciously change the way I spoke. Also, this was before social media and smartphones. There were no video calls. When people met online, their first real interaction was usually a phone call. This was the era when sizing up a person began with their voice.

It was during this time I remember discovering my lower register, and avoiding higher pitches altogether. I consciously spoke in a monotone voice, using only the lowest parts of my range, because I thought that's what sounded manly. To make matters worse, I started "frying" my voice. Not so much like the horrible vocal fry that became popular in 2012. This was a different kind of horrible. This was the I-just-woke-up-and-my-voice-is-husky voice that some men like to do when they want to sound sexy. Sometimes I would force a coughing fit prior to speaking to someone on the phone, just so my voice would be hoarse and easier to fry. Oh, the lengths we'll go to be accepted.

Fast forward a few more years, and I would start settling into a more authentic voice. It was no longer the soft, high-pitched voice I had in my teens, but it also wasn't the overly done *bassy* voice I used in my early 20s. It had leveled off somewhere in the middle. It was better than it had ever been, but still needed some work.

When I started training as an actor, I worked several times a week with a voice and speech coach over the course of many months. That was when I started treating my voice like an instrument. I discovered I could do so much more with it than I'd ever imagined. So many parts of my voice had remained unexplored until then. I began to develop and love my own voice for the first time in my life. Like any great musician, with practice comes greatness. Stop practicing and you get rusty, and your instrument will likely need some tuning. I can always hear and feel the difference in my own voice when I've done the exercises in this chapter diligently for a few days or weeks. It's clear, powerful and there's no nasality or hoarseness.

In this chapter, I'm going to share with you some of the ways I learned to develop a confident and powerful voice. Yes, it's also going to simultaneously make your voice more masculine by some people's standards. The information I'm sharing is a summary of the principles of powerful speech that I've learned from multiple vocal experts over the years, tailored to align with the purpose of this book. I recommend you get in the habit of recording yourself and listening back objectively when you're ready to implement the techniques you learn here. It's one of the best ways to measure progress. And I *highly* recommend a few sessions with a voice and speech coach if you've never worked with one before.

BUT, YOU DO HAVE POWER

Ever see someone command the attention of a room without shouting and without a microphone? You've probably seen this happen at a large dinner table at a holiday gathering, in a classroom, or during a meeting amongst work colleagues. There's always one person who can shut everyone else up when they speak. What is it about their voice that makes it powerful enough to cut through space and ambient noise and reach everyone in the room? The foundation of a powerful voice is in the breath and resonance and the ability to use the two to reach your audience. It comes from the core of the body and vibrates outward so the listener feels it. It commands their attention, but doesn't impose.

Practice these next three steps and hopefully you'll never again have to feel like you don't stand a chance at getting a word in at your rambunctious family dinner, or wave your hand in a roomful of opinionated colleagues at a discussion table as you shout obnoxiously "Can I say something!!?" Nah, I think you're ready to put those days behind you.

Find your diaphragm. Your voice box is in your throat, so why is the power deep down in the belly area and not the throat? Because the sounds made by the voice box are from the vibrations of the vocal cords as the breath passes through them. The more breath means the more vibration, and breath is powered by the diaphragm. The diaphragm is a muscle attached to the bottom of your rib cage, all the way around it. When you breathe, the ribs expand outward and the diaphragm sort of pushes your guts downward, opening up the belly area for the breath. Since the diaphragm is a muscle, it can stretch, which can allow for more expansive breathing. Think of it like a spring; the more you expand it downward, the more powerfully it springs back into place projecting the breath back out. This is what people mean when they say "speak from your diaphragm."

My personal favorite way to show my guys how to access their diaphragm is to imagine their lungs being in their belly, and trying to blow up their belly like a balloon. You can do this laying down, sitting or standing. Place your hands on your sides just below your rib cage. Take a deep breath and try to imagine sending the breath all the way down to your hands and expanding them outward. The more your sides expand outward, the more you're using your diaphragm. Breathing this way is one of the foundations for a powerful voice.

Posture also plays an important part in using your diaphragm properly. If you slouch when standing or sitting, forward or backward or to one side, you are inhibiting your ribs from fully expanding. Remember, the ribs are not only in the front of our body. They expand in all directions when we breathe, and the best way to allow for full range of motion is to sit and stand upright and aligned. Tension will also inhibit rib movement, so take 5-10 minutes to stretch your sides, back, chest, even hips prior to practicing diaphragmatic breathing.

Resonate the mask. This is how you make your voice cut through crowds, other sounds, and reach people further away without the need to shout. This area is called the mask because it is literally the front of your face. To feel what I'm talking about, try stretching the "ng" sound. Say "bring" or "sing" and elongate the ending for five seconds. Those vibrations you feel are in the mask of your face. Resonance in the mask can be very powerful, but can also be quite nasal and high pitched. If you are working from your diaphragm, the resonance in the mask will send your voice forward with a lot of resonance. If you don't have the right breath support, it will sound all nasal without the power. Try again.

Play around with the different sounds by using the "ng" sound and eventually opening up to a vowel. Go back and forth between the two sounds. The opening and closing you feel as you do this is your soft palate moving up and down. Hear and feel the difference in sounds as the soft palate opens and blocks the nasal passageway. Pay attention to how the resonance moves and feels different. You will use these two sounds for different purposes. Later we will discuss when you'll want to close off the nasal passage, by opening the soft palate for a different sound.

Fill the room. It's not exactly about loudness, but then again, it kinda is. What I mean is that I don't want you to think loudness directly correlates with a powerful voice because you may be inclined to shout, which isn't necessary. Nonetheless, filling the space you're in with the appropriate volume is essential, so instead of thinking about loudness, think about using your diaphragm and mask to achieve the appropriate amount of power for the distance you need to reach. Think of it as a similar concept to a basketball player shooting a hoop from different parts of the court. It's not simply about good form; it's also about understanding the amount of force needed to reach the hoop. Too little and the ball bounces off the rim. Too great and the ball bounces off the backboard. With practice, you can do the same with your voice.

Bigger isn't better in this case. Too big a voice can sound self-indulgent or overcompensating and might distract your listener, taking away your power. Here's a way to practice. Sit in a chair in the center of your room. Place your hand about six inches away from your face and say "This is how big of a voice I need to reach you" to your hand. Yeah, imagine a person was that close to you and, still using diaphragmatic breathing, speak to them. How big or small do you need to be to reach them? You may notice less resonance and it may sound breathier. That's okay. That means the deep breathing is still there, but less voice is needed to reach your audience.

Now extend your hand as far out as you can and see how big you need your voice to be to reach it using the same sentence. You'll probably notice you need a little more voice and resonance. Play with these two distances for a bit, and then move on to something farther away. Choose a spot on the floor or an object in the room about six feet from you and try reaching it. Next try the wall in front of you. Now try the wall behind you, without turning toward it. You're going to need a bit more resonance for that. Finally, imagine the room is full of people and you need to reach all of them. Go for it. Keep the throat open and relaxed. You do not need any tension for this, just deep breath and the diaphragm. Resonate with the mask or try imagining the resonance coming from all sides of you.

Practice this often. You can use this exercise for warming your voice up as well. The voice is completely operated by muscles. Warming them up and stretching them out is essential to get the most out of your voice. The more you stretch a muscle, the more range of motion you have. Let's see how we can apply that to your pitch.

GO AHEAD, ADD A LITTLE BASS

A lot of men who complain of not having a masculine voice are unhappy with the pitch of their voice. Basically, they tell me that they wish it was deeper and more commanding. While it's important we remember to accept what we have, we can certainly explore some ways to ensure we are using *all* of what we have. You're probably not using your full vocal range, and likely have some habits that are preventing you from accessing your lower register properly. What I mean is, yes, I think you *can* have a deeper voice (and still sound authentic).

Train your voice box. You've likely heard the terminology "muscle memory" used a few times before. While muscles do not actually have their own brain, it suggests that once a particular muscle group has been trained with some frequency, it will become second nature to access those muscles without needing to think about it because the muscle "remembers." The voice box, also known as the larynx or phonatory system if you want to be a fancy pants, is where sounds are produced. Because this organ is largely made up of elastic muscle tissue known as your vocal cords, it can be stretched and trained like other muscles. And it will also "remember."

Start by opening the soft palate. In the section on resonating the mask, we played around with opening and closing the soft palate. A closed soft palate will open up the nasal passage, producing a higher, more nasal sound that can cut through a crowd. Here we want to block the nasal passage by keeping the soft palate open, allowing for deeper sounds. Start with elongating the "ng" sound in "bring" or "sing" and then open up to a vowel. Try looking in the mirror as you do it. Shine a light into your mouth if you need to and pay attention to the back of your throat as you make the different sounds. When you open up to a vowel sound, watch to see how much the back of the throat lifts and opens. The more the better. For some, a wider mouth makes it easier to open the soft palate. One of my teachers says the best way to open the soft palate is to imagine a doctor checking out the back of our throat, holding your tongue down with a tongue depressor... now say "ahhh."

Now we need to warm-up your voice and focus on the lower register. The idea is to access the depth we're not using and give it a workout. Your lower register is probably deeper than you think it is, but we want to make sure that you're creating the sounds without gripping the throat. Tucking the chin down and gripping the throat creates a "fake" deep voice and ultimately hurts your vocal cords. Try it a couple times so you know what not to do. Consciously keep your head upright and your neck aligned with your spine to avoid this. You can also do this lying down on your back.

Using diaphragmatic breathing and an open soft palate, start with a vowel sound at the top of your breath until the breath runs out. On the next one, try going a little lower with the sound. Repeat. You can also start at the top of your breath and gradually drop lower and lower until the breath runs out. If you feel your throat gripping, you've gone too low. Recognize your limit and accept it. Continue with this, using deep breaths and eventually switch to different vowel sounds. Once you've made your way through all of the vowels, take a break if you need to or grab some water. How's the throat feeling? If you've kept it open and relaxed, you should not feel any strain. If you do, simply note it and be mindful going forward that the throat stays more relaxed. You may also notice the need to clear your throat several times throughout this exercise. That's a good thing! This will definitely clear some of the moisture out of your lungs.

When you're ready, have at it again and this time try to do a bit of a vocal rollercoaster – all vowel sounds and up and down with the pitch. *"Ooooeeeeeaaaaaauuuuiiiiiaaaaahhh."*

Let the sound *slowly* move from the highest part of your register to the lowest part of your register and back up and down. Start at the top of your breath, go for as long as you can, then take another breath and repeat. Do this several times, focusing on working out the lower part of your register. The more you practice using your lower register, the more easily you can access it when speaking, creating new vocal habits.

Lastly, use words. "I am creating new vocal habits by working out the lower register of my natural voice." Remember, up and down with the pitch. Play around. Last thing we want is to create a habit of being monotone. Monotone is considered manly by some. However, listen to any great male speakers and you'll hear plenty of musicality in their pitch as a way to keep the interest of their listeners, sound relatable and also reachable.

Lengthen words to stress them rather than using up-speak or upward inflection. This is important especially professionally. There have been a lot of articles written about up-speak in the workplace and how it makes one appear green and, well, annoying. What is it? It's ending sentences on a high note, specifically when it is not necessary. For example, say these following sentences aloud:

Declaration: I like coffee in the morning.
Question: Would you like a cup of coffee?

A lot of people will end a question with an upward inflection. It suggests inquisition and that a response is awaited. Try ending the following declarations with an upward inflection:

I like coffee in the morning.
I'd like to work toward a promotion.
I'm not really happy with this outcome.

How did you feel as you said each sentence? Doubtful? Condescending? Sarcastic? Passive? Passive-aggressive? Using an upward inflection when it isn't necessary can be perceived a number of ways, and oftentimes not positively. If you catch yourself doing it, try to make a conscious effort to end on a lower note. It will likely sound more confident and more direct. The same applies when emphasizing or stressing a word in a sentence. Instead of using a higher pitch, try elongating the word you want to stress.

Huskiness is wack when it's forced. I'm hearing a lot of guys doing this lately and it drives me nuts. Sure, if you have a naturally husky voice, use it to your advantage; if you don't, please don't try to sound like Batman by making your voice hoarse. You're probably not going to sound tough or sexy. You're probably just going to sound like you're doing something unnatural with your voice and overcompensating for something. Hoarseness will happen on its own when you wake up in the morning dehydrated or after excessive shouting. Huskiness may happen if you smoked or drank for years or strained your voice over a long period of time. A lot of lead vocalists of rock bands have a husky voice from years of strain. Yeah, it sounds great. It has a natural quality to it similar to a worn pair of jeans that tell a story and say, "I've been through a lot." Try to manufacture it without the history, however, and it'll likely seem like a fraudulent copy. Raspiness is a natural speaking quality some people have or don't have. Attempt any of these and you're playing a character, and without the acting chops, you're probably doing a piss-poor job. Own the voice you have. Take care of your voice by doing the exercises described here and treat it like both an instrument and a muscle. It will keep your voice clear, smooth, and powerful. Strain it for effect and you'll see that over time it will become weaker and weaker. Rather than huskiness, focus on resonance. You'll reach more people and hit them in their core.

BE GENEROUS = BE HEARD

When you speak, do you really want to be heard? Or is there some part of you that's holding back, protecting yourself? Maybe it's because you don't like your voice or you don't think what you're saying is important. Maybe it's because you're shying away from asserting your honest opinion. Or maybe you're telling yourself that people aren't listening, so you become self-conscious as you speak.

Any of these feelings, conscious or subconscious, can lead you to speaking too quickly, too softly, mumbling your words, covering your mouth as you're speaking and otherwise not being heard. Generosity can solve this. Consciously practicing generosity as you speak means *giving* your words. It means being willing to be exposed and being willing to be heard.

"Here, I give you my words. I give them generously."

That can be the message to self before you speak from now on. There's a kind of selflessness in it. It takes the focus off of you and puts it on the other person. Take them in and acknowledge that they are hoping and waiting to *receive* from you. Your objective is to *give* to them. Be generous. If ever you find yourself overwhelmed or self-conscious trying to focus on too many vocal technicalities at once, you can fall back on this one. Give. It's an act of generosity and courage.

Here are some additional ways you can better be heard. These little details can make a huge difference in how confident you sound.

Slow down. Take. Your. Time. What you may think is too slow probably isn't. Record yourself reading something at varying speeds and note which felt most comfortable and which felt too fast or too slow. Play it back and imagine it's someone else reading to you. Pay attention as you listen to which pace you think sounds best and whether or not it's consistent with how you felt as you read it. I have noticed that men tend to speak slower. This is perhaps due to more controlled expression or less emotion behind the words. Heightened emotions could make someone speak with more excitement and faster. I'm not saying you need to suck all of the emotion out of your speech. You can be passionate about what you are saying and still maintain a pace that feels deliberate and understandable.

Finish your sentences. Dropping the ends of sentences is a common speech quirk, and often a sign that the speaker doesn't actually want to be heard or is feeling self-conscious. Finish your sentences with the same amount of breath and voice that you began with, especially if the last word of a sentence is one that needs to be stressed. Hit the end for emphasis and take a pause or breath before you begin your next sentence. To maintain a good rhythm, don't pause after every sentence. That could sound annoying. Do, however, make it a point to finish your thoughts!

How long is the sentence you're about to say? How much breath will it require to get through it? Will I need to take a breath in the middle of the sentence to be certain I finish the thought with enough voice? Practice this while reading something aloud. You won't be able to think about these things as you speak in day-today life. Practicing at home will help create the habit of breathing when necessary and finishing your sentences. All of your words are important.

Allow yourself pauses. I have a habit of saying "um" when I speak. Vocalized pauses fill the silence as we gather our thoughts and choose our next words. When we do it, we are essentially sharing our internal process with the listener, and it's not necessary. It rarely adds anything valuable to what we're saying. When speaking publicly, I'm usually rehearsed on the material I'm sharing and it happens less. In day-to-day speech, however, I tend to vocalize my pauses. That is something I'm working on doing less. I don't feel the need to remove it completely from casual speech, because there's an authenticity to it; but too much can be distracting and sound like uncertainty or self-doubt.

If we consciously allow ourselves pauses – to find our place as we read, present information or gather our thoughts – it could help remove these self-conscious, unnecessary space fillers. Silent pauses are generally well accepted. Taking a pause to gather our thoughts or find our place is often viewed by listeners as a deliberate part of the speech. They usually will not see our inner process and won't know we needed a moment to think. In fact, there can be power in what seems like a deliberate pause. It says "I want what I previously said to land. I would like you to take a moment to process it because it's important." Instead of diluting your speech with vocalized pauses, empower it by giving yourself permission to remain silent as needed.

Enunciate. I grew up in New Jersey. I say *gonna* instead of *going to* and *lemme* instead of *let me*, and I often drop the *g* at the end of *ing* words. *Ey, whatta ya doin?* When speaking casually to people with whom we're comfortable, especially people who have similar speech patterns to our own, I think it's okay to speak with our natural inclinations. Many of us feel like it's a part of our identity. Enunciation skills will come in handy in your professional life when you need to read something aloud, during times you're feeling uncomfortable or self-conscious, or when saying words you've never said before or don't say often like professional jargon.

Enunciation comes from the Latin word *enuntiationem*, meaning "declaration." It basically means pronouncing words clearly. Besides knowing the correct way the words we use are pronounced, the best way to become skilled at enunciating is to get the mouth used to saying all of the consonants and vowel sounds of your language. My favorite way to do that is by practicing tongue twisters. Get a book of tongue twisters or find some online and repeat them as part of your daily ritual. Switch them up once you become good at them!

Something else to note is how you use your articulators when you enunciate. Articulators are any of the vocal organs above the larynx, including the tongue, lips, teeth, and hard palate. I mentioned earlier that I have noticed that women tend to use their articulators more than men do, resulting in a more expressive mouth when they speak. That does not mean you shouldn't use yours or be articulate when you speak. You can be articulate without looking like you're eating your words. Think about articulating downward with your mouth rather than to the sides and the movements will be more subtle. When practicing at home, let your mouth move freely, specifically if enunciation is an area that needs significant improvement. Get your mouth and articulators in the habit of moving and stretching. You can always scale it back later.

Crafting your voice is like learning to play a new instrument. Practice is great, but you will probably only get better if you are practicing playing it *correctly*. That means understanding your instrument on a technical level and accepting what it can and cannot do. Your instrument is unique. Making it sound more masculine is relative to what you think the qualities of masculinity are. Perhaps focus on achieving each one of those individual qualities rather than striving for what you think is the ideal masculine voice. You *can* make your voice more powerful by learning how to deepen your breath and access your diaphragm. You *can* make your voice deeper by working out your full vocal range with daily warm-ups. You *can* make your speech more convincing through practicing generosity and a conscious willingness to be heard.

The following story uses every vowel and consonant sound in the English language. My vocal coach had me memorize it and say it aloud daily, enunciating each word. You can do the same and use it to implement all of the other exercises that apply to you in this chapter. Memorize it so you can say it anywhere. Every day you practice, your instrument gets stronger.

Eleven benevolent elephants met Lily and Lucy in Philadelphia and went to see Camelot in unique New York with guns and drums and drums and guns, which they kept in a bodega bodega bodega. They walked for miles and miles and miles until they saw Manny and Nancy, who danced hand in hand in the sand as they sang, "Many a moon, many a moon, many a moon."

They came across brilliant Italian William from Topeka, who kept murmuring, "Mommala Poppala Mommala Poppala." They begged him to join them. "Will you, William? Will you, William? Will you,

William? Can't you, won't you, don't you, William? Did you, would you, could you, William?"

William simply said, "Lilli Lolli Lilli Lolli." Then round the rugged rock the ragged rascal ran, to be among Culligan and calla lilies, to let his tone hum down as easily as a sigh.

NOTES

NOTES

CRAFTING
MASCULINITY
Ch8: Regulating Emotions
(self-regulation)

Men I work with often ask me "How do I perform better under pressure or work at the top of my game through periods of stress, depression, or anxiety? How do I become more like the guys who can remain poised and even-keeled in heightened life situations?" Emotional regulation, buddy. Since actors are often masters of emotional regulation, in this chapter, I'll be sharing several of the techniques I learned in the years I spent acting. I use these techniques in both my personal and professional life, and teach them in coaching.

I consider emotional regulation a form of self-temperance that allows us to control how we experience our emotions and how our emotions influence our behavior. Can you think of any tasks that are significantly more difficult to perform when we are overwhelmed with nervousness or anxiety? You might think of taking a final exam, speaking in front of people, a first date, or a job interview. All of those can be anxiety-inducing. Emotional regulation can lessen the severity of that anxiety so that you can stay present and be less self-conscious during those times. It can also be useful during bouts of frustration, discouragement, or sadness that can affect our ability to function and get through our day. While we most likely won't be able to remove the internal programming that set off these emotional responses, we *can* neutralize or counterbalance it with new programming in that crucial window between emotion and action. We can learn to reduce the intensity of the emotions through rationalizing and produce better actions for better outcomes. That is why men who can emotionally regulate often make great managers and leaders – they remain practical and logical in high-stakes circumstances.

Another great benefit of emotional regulation is it can lead to having more fulfilling, deeper experiences of the positive emotions and joys in life. It's as much about letting yourself luxuriate in your feelings as it is lessening the negative effects of them. Feelings can be one of the greatest joys in life. Let's be clear: emotional regulation is never about numbing feelings!

Absolutely not.

Denying your feelings is the antithesis of moderation, and unfortunately a default way a lot of men have been taught to handle their emotions. Let's get a better understanding of why so many men suppress their feelings and the role society has played in perpetuating that. It's central to the discussion of masculinity today and a lot of what's covered in this chapter.

MASCULINITY + EMOTIONS

Society's need to suppress men's emotions has likely been happening since the beginning of humanity and has evolved right along with us. Today, however, the suppression seems to come from two conflicting points of view producing a no-win situation for us.

Lose the anger. In my experience, it would make sense that testosterone, a hormone we know to be produced in much higher levels in boys than girls, might be linked to aggressive behavior in men. Aggression may have served humanity well when men needed to protect their family from danger, hunt for food, or fight for their land. You might even say that this aggression was a major contributor to the survival of humanity. However, if we look at history and statistics today, you could say that men's aggressive temperament is also responsible for the vast majority of violent crimes in the world. Since we're no longer living in conditions where this aggression would benefit mankind, would it be a seemingly logical solution that we teach men to suppress emotions associated with violence... such as anger? Nope. Anger is a human emotion that we all feel and it needs to be released in a healthy way. Denying or suppressing anger can lead to shame, guilt, depression, and even uncontrollable violent outbursts.

Lose the tears. My work, along with findings from numerous studies, has led me to believe that most women inherently have higher levels of empathy than most men. Those with higher empathy have a greater ability to nurture others, understand the needs of others, and express themselves. When it comes to interpersonal relationships, raising children, and providing emotional support, those are positive qualities, but what about in conditions when men were required to hunt, fight, and protect? Having high empathy could actually inhibit a man's ability to do those things. In that case, men might have been discouraged from showing signs of empathy or high sensitivity, such as crying, to avoid weakening their ability to purposefully hunt, fight, and protect their families. When that same archaic thinking is applied in modern times, we have a problem. Why are men still being taught that they shouldn't cry or express sadness or pain?

There you have it. The inevitable lose-lose battle we face:

Don't express anger as it leads to violence, crime, and war, but don't be vulnerable, either, as it is unmanly and weak.

And precisely why this chapter is so important. My goal is to neutralize that programming. I want to teach men how to regulate their emotions in a way that is practical and positive so they can feel focused, clear-headed and in control, and still have the ability to be a joyful, expressive, sappy mush without any self-judgment. Please take what you learn here and apply it however the fuck feels right for you, because in the end we're probably going to be criticized either way. Okay, let's dive in!

EMOTIONAL AWARENESS, CAPICHE?

Emotional regulation is commonly confused with emotional intelligence. While they are components of one another, they are not synonyms. Of the most commonly defined components of emotional intelligence, it's self-awareness that I believe is the most important contributor to and prerequisite for emotional regulation. Self-awareness covers the conscious knowledge of the *entire* self; but for our purposes, we want you to focus your awareness specifically on the *emotional* self. It's not entirely self-awareness or emotional intelligence; it's kinda... *emotional awareness.* Let's distill it down to something simpler:

When + What + Why = Emotional Awareness

Awareness of your emotions is basically the ability to identify when, what, and why you're feeling something. Figuratively speaking, it's a muscle that gets stronger and stronger as you practice using it through conscious assessments. Once you develop the skill, you will be able to effectively assess your emotions and then determine whether or not they should guide you to an action.

Emotional awareness can be used when you are experiencing positive or negative emotions. While some of us may have difficulty identifying and processing positive feelings, more men struggle with the negative ones, and so I've decided to focus on those times. We'll get into positive emotions later in the chapter.

Look for clues, Holmes (when). The first step is to learn to recognize *when* you're feeling something that might need your assessment or intervention. You need to play a little bit of a detective here, putting pieces together and finding patterns in your own feelings and behaviors. Answer these questions to help you better identify patterns and find clues:

Is there any common denominator in circumstances where I've felt something that led to irrational or detrimental action? Who or what were they?

These things could be triggers. Knowing your triggers will help you avoid them in the future and prepare you for the emotion that follows, giving you a heads up that it might soon be time to stop and assess.

When I feel my emotions, where do I feel them physically?

Try to imagine situations where you remember feeling anger, sadness, joy, or any other emotion you remember feeling intensely. Can you physicalize it right now and imagine yourself there again? What happens when you do? Do you feel hot? Cold? Does your heart race? Do you get a tightness in your chest or feel your breathing shorten? Does your face get flushed or do your legs shake? Do you feel a sinking feeling in your gut? The body often physically lets us know when something is going on emotionally that needs to be addressed. Knowing how different emotions affect you physically is a great start to knowing when it might be time for an emotional assessment.

Are there any specific behaviors that I know have been a direct response to certain emotions?

For example, do you touch or scratch your head when you are uncomfortable, crack your knuckles when you're nervous, cross your arms when you're annoyed, ball up your fists when you're angry, tap or fidget when you're losing your patience? Catching yourself before or even after behaviors such as these will be an opportunity for you to assess the precipitating emotion.

Go out into the world with your sensors ready to spot them. A heightened level of consciousness is going to be needed for a while. Conscious awareness, whether you tie a piece of string around your finger, set reminders in your phone, or repeat things to yourself through out the day is what leads to discoveries, understanding, and eventually a more secondary, subconscious awareness.

Stop and assess the mess (what). Once you've heightened your awareness to the point that you can recognize *when* you're feeling something that needs to be assessed, you're ready to go one layer deeper and identify *what* you're feeling. As soon as you recognize an emotion bubbling up in you that requires your attention, stop. Yes, the first and most important part here is to find a way to stop. I don't mean stop the feeling; I mean interrupt the process smack in the middle of emotion and action–this is the crucial window where you'll eventually get to input some new programming. Granted, you won't always be able to stop what you're in the middle of doing and take 10 minutes to assess your inner wiring. The times when you can are going to be your practice right now. With practice, you will eventually be able to do this in 10 seconds in the middle of an emotionally heightened circumstance.

What am I feeling? Ask yourself and do the best you can to identify the emotion. This requires wisdom and courage. Your wisdom here is your intuition. Go through different emotions in your head until you reach the one that you think is closest to what you're feeling, and then trust your intuition.

Your courage is your honesty with yourself. You need to be willing to admit to yourself that you're feeling fear, envy, jealousy, sadness, humiliation, despair or whatever. Be fucking honest with yourself! These are human emotions and we all feel them. You might be feeling several at once. Do the best you can to identify each emotion. It doesn't matter if you're right. You might decide later that you weren't, and that's cool. Like anything, you'll get better at this the more you do it.

Validate yourself, dammit (why). Time for a little self-love and compassion. This is yet another layer deeper into your guts and inner emotional workings. Once you know *what* you're feeling, the next step is to identify *why* you're feeling it. It will lead you to a deeper understanding of yourself, and most importantly, empower you with the ability to determine whether or not you should let the emotion guide you to action. Why am I feeling this? What happened that made me respond with this feeling? What meaning have I given the external stimulus that led me to this feeling? Do your best here. Look for clues and patterns and dig into your core for answers. Am I feeling jealous because I wanted the promotion my friend got? Am I feeling rejected because I didn't get the response I was hoping for. Am I feeling humiliated because I think my brother intentionally challenged me in front of the whole family? Am I feeling discouraged because I feel like my work isn't as good as my peer's and I'm comparing myself? You might feel uncomfortable as you do this. It might make you cringe and squirm. Trust the process, brother. No one else knows what's going on inside you and no one else can see your process, so be as raw and truthful with yourself as you can. Validate your feeling by telling yourself it's okay to feel that way. Be good to yourself here. Talk to yourself as if you're the big brother to a younger you. Your honesty and compassion are what'll lead you to *why*. Then and only then can you make the call as to whether or not the emotion should guide your next action.

FIND THE OBJECTIVE

If through using your emotional awareness you've determined an emotion should not guide your next action or you're just not sure, how can you determine what action *will* be suitable? You have to find the objective. Identifying the objective of a circumstance is a foolproof way to produce the action that is most likely to get you the outcome you want.

Time for a little acting!

In most acting methods, there are three very basic questions the actor needs to answer before he can do anything else. These three questions are the fundamental truths and foundation of the scene that the actor will build upon.

Who am I?
Who am I talking to?
What do I want?

Answering the first question tells the actor who the character is that he's playing. His line might be, "Hey kid, come here," and the way he says it largely depends on who he is. Is he a cop, a school teacher, a gangster, or a circus clown? Go ahead, try saying the line differently for all four characters! It's fun. In life, we can ask ourselves this same question. Who am I: a peer, authority, student, mentor? It'll help us choose which side of ourselves we want to call upon or which hat we want to wear for a situation. It will affect our energy, tone, and actions.

Answering the second question tells the actor what his relationship is with his scene partner. His line might be, "Wanna play?" Is he speaking to his wife, his child, his poker buddy, or his enemy? Can you see how it can mean four different things depending on who he's speaking to? Go for it. Give all four your best shot. Like the first question, this can also be used in several different life scenarios. For example, would you set a boundary with your boss the same way you'd set one with a child? Of course not. Would you speak to a room full of single moms the same way you would to a group of adolescent boys? I hope not.

Answering the third question tells the actor his objective in the scene. What does he want from the other character in the scene? Take the line, "Come with me, I have something to show you," and consider how differently it would be said based on these three possible objectives:

-You want your scene partner to cower in fear for their life.
-You want your scene partner to get sexually aroused.
-You want your scene partner to buy a car from you.

Funny, right? The same line can mean three very different things depending on the objective. Of all three questions actors ask themselves when initially handed a script, this is the one that can be applied to the most life circumstances. We can and should ask ourselves this question in life constantly: what do I want?

When in doubt, use your values. In acting, the objective is almost always provided by the writer. Sometimes, the actor will need to read the entire script, searching for patterns and clues in order to find the objective of just one scene. Other times, it'll be right in his face. In life, the objective is determined by you and only you. This puts you completely in control, but can also put an immense amount of pressure on you. *What do I want* could become *what should I want* or *what do I want right now* or *what am I going to want later?* When you're in a scenario where what you want isn't crystal clear, refer to your values and try to find the objective that aligns most with them.

Prepare when possible. Habitually ask yourself what your objective is before doing anything important, whether it's an interview or a first date. Knowing your objective in advance saves you from needing to make the assessment in the moment. Thinking about it in advance gives you time to be detailed and specific about the outcome you want. Specificity is going to make you stand out! For example, going into an interview with the objective of getting the job is general and most likely not going to make you stand out from any other interviewee. Everybody wants the job, not to mention, it's not often we leave an interview with a job offer so your objective is hardly achievable. However, if your objective is for the hiring manager to see that you are the most knowledgeable candidate of the company's mission, you will have something much more specific to prepare. Same goes for a first date. A general objective might be that you want to be liked. That's not unique and might even lead to clumsy, desperate behavior. If you make your objective to get your date to laugh, to dance or to feel special, you'll have something specific to prepare.

Can this be done in the moment without time to prep? It can, with practice. Every time you practice this in advance, the process will be stored in your mental arsenal and can be called upon in future scenarios that require you to improvise.

IDENTIFY THE ACTION

You've validated your feelings and found your objective. Now it's time to choose an action to achieve it. Learning about actions was a game changer for me. It helped solve one of my biggest life challenges: working through emotions that don't align with my objective. For example, if I'm feeling nervous, how am I going to achieve an objective that requires an act of confidence? Actions saved me during those times.

Actions are simply the act of doing something. If we repeat an action enough, we become good at it, and we can do it despite how we're feeling. Check this out. If I tell you to do jumping jacks, can you? Probably. You've likely done them several times so your body has it programmed into its memory bank. If you were feeling depressed and tired, you could still do jumping jacks if you *had* to, correct? You might not feel like doing them, but you could. Same goes for a situation where you're feeling nervous, uncomfortable, and self-conscious - you could still do jumping jacks if you absolutely *had* to. Jumping jacks are an action. When you fully commit to doing your best jumping jacks, you can do them at any time regardless how you're feeling because you've done them so many times before. The same goes for any other action that's been practiced enough times.

Let's use a previous example. You're going to a job interview and you determine your objective is to show the hiring manager that you are the most knowledgeable candidate of the company's mission. You're going to need to choose a specific action in order to achieve that objective. Let's say the action you choose is to passionately detail a previous work experience where you responded in a manner that's nicely in alignment with the company's mission. The action here is to *passionately detail*. Try to recall a time in your life when you've passionately detailed something. If you've repeated this action enough times in your life, you'll be able to re-access it like riding a bike. Now take the focus off what you're feeling and ride that fucking bike. You could be nervous, self-conscious, and squeezing your ass cheeks trying not to shit yourself and still passionately detail in that interview. You can do this for any action you've repeated enough times. Just like finding the objective, if there's any important situation in life for which you have time to prepare, identifying and practicing your action in advance is always going to produce better results. This will also give you the option to choose actions that aren't yet accessible in the heat of the moment. Repetition is key.

Getting from the emotion to a suitable action might seem like a complicated process that will take an impractical amount of time to implement, but it really isn't. Like anything new, in the beginning it'll be a little messy and that's okay. New skills get better over time with practice, and life provides us with tons of opportunities to practice this. The more you practice in advance, the faster you'll be able to revisit the process in the moment when needed. It can be used in heightened circumstances and also day-to-day life experiences. This entire process can be done when you're brushing your teeth in the morning and suddenly feel a jolt of annoyance that you don't want to take with you through the rest of the day. Practice it in multiple circumstances. Every time you effectively navigate from an emotion to a suitable action, you'll store that objective and that action in your mental toolbox for future use. You'll be surprised how many times you use the same ones in paralleled life situations.

UP-REGULATION, WOOHOO!

We worked through how to down-regulate or minimize the intensity of a heightened emotional experience. Now let's look at the times you may want to up-regulate or increase the intensity of an emotion. How about when you're in the middle of a challenging physical workout that's kicking your ass? How do you channel the excitement, confidence, anger or whatever feeling you need to power through the challenge? You might blast your favorite get-amped song, start talking yourself up, or think of something that excites you. That's up-regulation. We've all done it at one point or another. Unfortunately, we can't always take a break in the middle of certain high-stakes life situations to up-regulate or generate a feeling we want. We can, however, do an emotional preparation beforehand. The most common emotion the men I've worked with want to up-regulate is confidence, so that's the one I'm going to show you how to self-generate. You can prep on any emotion using this process.

Your emotional preparation is done at home prior to whatever circumstance or event you need the emotion for. Get yourself somewhere comfortable where you'll have no distractions. Lay on a rug or a mat, ideally wearing loose, comfortable clothing, and start by letting go of any unnecessary tension with a few minutes of stretches and deep breaths. Give yourself permission to let go of all other thoughts, and relax.

When was a time you felt super confident? Think about it and see if you can take yourself back to a recent experience. If nothing comes to mind, scan each area of life. Try to remember a time at work, among peers, in class, at the gym, out with friends, at home, even in the bedroom when you achieved something great... when you impressed yourself or others and were praised for it... a time you just knew you did a great job. Go back into your past if necessary and don't be afraid to use sex when possible. Sex-related memories that generate confidence can add a playfully mischievous twinkle in the eye that says "I have a secret and you don't know what it is" and can work nicely even in nonsexual circumstances. If you can't think of a specific time, then create one with your imagination where you're feeling confident... like through-the-roof-confidence. Be specific with people, places, and things as you build it. Your visualization does not have to have anything to do with your upcoming circumstance or event. It just needs to generate a feeling of great confidence.

Connect yourself emotionally to the visualization, whether real or imaginary, by playing it like a movie in your mind. The more details, the better. Let it slowly build up to that awesome moment of achievement when you were radiating with confidence. Let yourself feel it all over. Go ahead and smile. It should feel good. In what part of your body do you feel it the most? Chest, belly, face, fingers, toes? Live out the scenario a few times over. Once you're fully connected to the feeling, emotionally and physically, bring it to a standing position and move around with it. Let it energize you!!!

Can you think of a specific song that could be the soundtrack to this visualization? It has to be a song that gets you moving. It doesn't matter how cheesy or over-the-top it is. If it works, use it. Play it *loudly*. Use your headphones if you have thin walls. Move around. Physicalize it. Throw a punch in the air. Play air guitar. Be an idiot. No one can see you, so have fun! Can you think of a narrative for all of this? You have the visualization and you have the soundtrack. What are some words that will reinforce the confidence? Play around.

"I'm a beast!"
"I'm a badass!"
"I got this!"
"Who's the man?"

Be as gratuitous as you want. Don't be modest or humble. Don't be the grown-up right now. This is the time to be free and instinctive. Be animalistic. Be a kid! Be a douchebag! Find words that do something to you and say them aloud. Keep trying until you end up with the perfect word or phrase that lights you up.

Once you have successfully self-generated confidence through your visualization, music, and words, let yourself live it out for a while. Enjoy it. It can be five minutes or you can go longer, just don't exhaust yourself. You want to save some of that energy for the upcoming circumstance or event you need it for. Remember, emotions are ephemeral – they come and go just like that. You might not be able to generate the same level of confidence at your event as you did during your prep. That's okay. If you truly connected with the feeling, you will be able to re-access some of it on your big day. Start the day with the same emotional prep. Bring your headphones and play your song on your way to the event. Say the associated words or phrases aloud or in your head. The music and words will act as direct links to your visualization and the feeling of confidence. Do your best to regenerate it right before you walk in the door, then drop it and forget it. Do not focus on generating the feeling in the middle of your event. Trust the work you did and be present. Some of that confidence is there and *will* show, even if accompanied by nerves.

THE LICENSE TO FEEL GOOD

Do you look down or away or cover your face when you laugh? Do you create tension in your lips or contort your mouth to avoid a full smile? Have you ever taken your hand and literally wiped the smile off your face? You may be subconsciously blocking yourself from feeling good.

I've seen a lot of men struggle to let themselves experience and express happiness, joy, love, excitement, and other positive emotions. I've noticed it throughout my life and it wasn't until I became a coach that I learned this usually only happens for two reasons: fear or guilt. These two culprits can manifest into several negative thinking patterns, a few of which I detail below along with offering some ways you can potentially counter them. These are not short-term fixes or preparations, but long-term rewiring. It takes time and patience to reconfigure old emotional circuitry. Some sessions with a therapist or coach might help the process.

Be willing to be vulnerable. Some guys think that letting themselves feel positive feelings temporarily lowers their defenses and makes them more susceptible to harm. They're absolutely right. Letting ourselves experience feelings like happiness and love disarms us and often involves some form of trust in another person. It exposes a raw side of us that we might be afraid to show because of how we will look or how others will perceive us. We become susceptible to the pains of rejection and loss. You have the choice to play it safe and stay off the highway, missing out on all the potentially positive experiences and connections that come with it, or you can take the risks and go for the ride, reminding yourself that, in most cases, the worst outcome is not insurmountable. The heart is tough.

Remind yourself you deserve to be happy. Sometimes, we will experience feelings of fear when happiness or joy stirs up inside us. This is usually linked to something from our past that we're struggling to move on from. A past where happiness was constantly distinguished by disappointment, loss, or betrayal can lead to inner programming that associates happiness with pain. It's the case of the abused dog that winces when you hand him a treat or reach out to pet him. He was taught to believe he doesn't deserve to be happy or isn't worthy of love.

It can also be survivor's guilt: an association with someone else's suffering, such as an unhappy parent, friend, or loved one, or the death of a loved one. Guilt can arise if we feel like our happiness has surpassed someone we care about, or if we see our happiness as a betrayal from mourning the death of a loved one.

The only way to get through these is to move on from your past. Moving on does not mean forgetting. It means learning to love yourself, giving yourself permission to heal, and allowing your story or memories to move forward with you. You *deserve* to be happy. *You* deserve to be happy.

Be willing to face pain. Happiness and pain are kind of a package deal. We can't numb one without numbing the other. Read that sentence again. If we allow ourselves to feel happiness, we're inevitably going to face more pain and vice versa. That is just how these fickle emotions work. The courage to face hurt, loss, or heartache builds resilience in us, but it also trains us to stop extinguishing positive emotions we may have been consciously or subconsciously denying ourselves from feeling.

"I'm going to allow myself to feel this positive feeling. I know it's a risk for it can lead to hurt, loss or heartache, but I'm willing to face that and overcome it."

That's been a powerful mantra for me. Use it or create one using your own words. The sooner we come to accept that pain is a part of life, the sooner we can start building a tolerance for it and braving the fear of it. And, the sooner we can be happy.

Feeling good looks good. Smiles and laughter are infectious. There are plenty of people out there that are attracted to men who smile, express joy, and have a good sense of humor. Just saying, dude.

PURGE

This is not specifically a reference to the movie franchise, but the concept is similar. I think we'd all be better off if we purged our feelings of rage, hate, hurt, resentment, jealousy, and all the other ugly feelings we don't like to admit we feel. But how? It's probably not a good idea to murder your boss or burn down your high school. Besides the fact that these actions are irreversible and have major consequences, they'd probably only make you feel better for a split second before you came back to your senses and realized you have completely betrayed your values. On the other hand, if you do nothing about the feelings, they don't usually just go away. They can build up inside you and become toxic, manifesting into self-defeating behaviors and sometimes even physical conditions. I've come to believe that even certain diseases can either be brought on or aggravated by an internal conflict or stress.

Purging feelings is no different than taking a shit. First, the body produces something that's meant to be released. Next, we release it and feel cleansed and lighter. If we hold onto it... well, that can get ugly. For this reason, I believe that channeling negative feelings in a healthy way is essential for emotional regulation. You need to start from a clean slate to have optimal clarity and control. These are some of my favorite ways to purge unreleased feelings. They've helped me big time.

Creative expression. I get it - not everyone is an artist and, for these purposes, you don't need to be technically skilled. This is not about making a handsome work of art. It's about expressing yourself and being as raw and uncensored as possible. For releasing rage, maybe pick up a pencil and write about the feeling or use your imagination to tell a story about a character meeting their grim demise. Whether or not the character represents a real person in your life is up to you. Be as detailed as you can. The same applies to drawing, acting, or any other creative medium. You can either choose to express yourself truthfully or to keep everything of the imaginary world, with characters and scenarios that represent your life and your feelings. The idea is to get it out and not hold back. Remember, you can shred it, burn it, delete it when you're done, or store it in a safe place where no one else has access. Don't judge yourself in this process. I have created some unbelievably dark pieces over the years.

Talking. It's underrated. Having a conversation or venting session with a good listener who you trust is a great way to purge feelings. A buddy, relative, or helping professional who can remain objective and not judge you can act as a sounding board for your thoughts. Sometimes you may not even want feedback, but simply need to get something off your chest that's been bothering you. Talking about it gets it out. You can do this over the phone, on a car ride together, sitting somewhere in nature, in your home with food and drinks, or even at a public place like a cafe, bar, or restaurant that's conducive for a private conversation. Trading talking and listening time is probably essential for most friendships, but depends on the relationship. You can also hire a coach or therapist specifically for this. You do not need to be in crisis to benefit from talking.

Physical aggression. Sometimes you really just need to be aggressive or fuck something up to get out some frustration and rage. You can use a punching bag, have an intense workout at the gym, start taking martial arts or boxing classes or, in some cities like New York, you can even pay to smash bottles, plates, and electronics in an enclosed space with weapons and safety gear! Physicalizing feelings of anger can be cathartic and I highly recommend it. It has left me feeling energized, liberated and sleeping better at night. We are animals and, men especially, seem to have an inherent need to be physically aggressive. More on this later.

Inducing a meltdown. I'm not going to spoon-feed you all the reasons why men should let themselves cry more often, but here's a few really good ones: it's one of the most efficient ways a human can release pent-up emotions, reduce stress levels, release endorphins, lower anxiety, and enhance their mood. And just like you pick your nose and squeeze a zit, this can be done in privacy and no one else needs to know about it but you. It might be time to face your fears of tears, bro. It's a part of life. I understand it may have been years since you've cried and you may be thinking that you've forgotten how or can't. I reached that point once. I'm going to share with you a few ways to produce tears that have worked for me. You might not succeed the first couple tries, but don't judge yourself and do not give up. Eventually you will put a crack in the wall you've built, whether it's one tear or a full on ugly-cry meltdown. It takes a lot of patience and determination to knock down a wall we may have spent years constructing. One tear means you loosened a brick, and that's a major victory.

Tear-jerker films or shows can be a great trigger for an emotional release. Sometimes, the easiest way to cry is when it's about something that has nothing to do with us. If you have a particular movie or show that tugs at your heart strings, start there. In the past you might have held back tears during the hardest scenes, but this time, let yourself give into it. See if it can lead you to thinking about a parallel in your own life. A few that get me every time I watch are *Old Yeller, The Green Mile* and *Shawshank Redemption*. You can also use videos of animal rescues, owners putting down a pet, success stories of people who came from a great struggle, or even material from specific events in history such as war, mass killings, or terrorist-attacks. Try music, too. It doesn't matter what you use as long as it plays on you enough to produce a healthy release of emotion. Find what works for you. You only need to use the material long enough to bring the emotions close to the surface. Then you can go make yourself comfortable somewhere to release it. Remember, nobody is too tough to cry. In fact, when I've used guided meditation and other methods to help men have a release, it's usually been the "toughest" ones to have the most powerful releases.

Emotional regulation is an internal process, but it works like a muscle. The more you use it, the stronger and more familiar it becomes. Like all other internal processes we discuss, it's about small steps, patience, and consistency.

It starts with emotional awareness and the ability to identify when, what, and why you're feeling something. Your feelings are valid and you can make it your job to always remind yourself.

Having a crystal-clear understanding of the objective of a life situation coupled with a keen emotional awareness is going to give you the ability to determine the action you want. Practice the hell out of your actions. They're a life saver!

We have the ability to generate emotions in ourselves when we need them in life. Emotional preparations are a great way to become familiar with emotions we need frequently throughout our lives. We can also learn to generate feelings of anger or sadness when it comes time to purge and release!

Regulating your emotions doesn't just make life a little happier, it puts you in control. It makes you the switchboard operator rather than the switchboard.

* *virtual fist bump* *

NOTES

NOTES

CRAFTING

MASCULINITY

Ch9: Bonding with Men

There are a lot of reasons why men need other men:

Validation. Some of my colleagues believe that praise and admiration are the number one motivators of men. I've noticed men tend to seek these two things from other men more often than they do from women. Men often rely on each other to be reminded that they are important, purposeful, and worthy.

Inspiration. Men can learn from each other and pick up each other's ways, mimicking and emulating those they look up to. They may feel inspired when they see other men doing something they see as admirable, saying to themselves, "If I practice that, maybe I can do it, too."

Competition. This can crossover with inspiration. Sometimes when men see other men doing something better than them, they become inspired but also use the other man's abilities as a benchmark for themselves, feeling the need to surpass them and be the bigger, smarter, faster, stronger man. Other times, the need to compete can be about the game, itself, and winning, rather than the need to better.

Honor. It has two contexts here: adherence to moral code and high respect or glory. The two may have reciprocal influence on each other, but they are different. When a man strives for high-respect status or significance of any kind, it's often measured by what other men think of him. Men often measure their adherence to moral code by the validation of other men as well.

Male-bonding. Everything mentioned above contributes to a unique, special bond when men connect and befriend one another.

Masculinity. It is frequently celebrated, exercised, and boldly showcased when men are in the company of other men.

You may have read some of those reasons and thought to yourself, "that doesn't sound like a good thing." I hear you. I didn't say it was. Objectively, I gave you the reasons I believe men need other men in their life based on my personal experiences and the parallels I've seen in the men I've worked with. Like everything else in life, there are positives and equal and opposite negatives to how men relate to other men. We're going to get into a lot of that in this chapter, but it's all with the intention to encourage you to bond with other men. It was such an important part of my journey. As I noted in the first chapter, I didn't have many strong male relationships growing up. It wasn't until I became a resident at an all-boys facility that I was inspired to call upon my own masculinity. In many ways, I felt I was forced to - it was either adapt or live each day in fear. Sometimes, the best way to learn is to dive in headfirst... or in my case, be thrown in. I'm grateful I was thrown into that environment! It was the starting point to becoming the man I always wanted to be, and, no matter how uncomfortable it makes you, I believe with every fiber of my being that connecting with other men is an essential part of the journey to crafting masculinity. I do not recommend a boys home, prison or a street gang - although, in some aspects, those are optimal environments for crafting your masculinity - but I do see value in exploring healthy ways to put yourself in a sink-or-swim environment with other men. I'll mention a few of those ways throughout the chapter as I detail what I learned in my own experiences in group settings with other men.

MALE BONDING + ADVERSITY

Men appear to have the most meaningful connections through adversity. At least that's been my experience… and a few rats, too. I once read that a study performed on male rats showed that when the rats were exposed to a stressful environment, they became more social and they connected with one another. They showed increased levels of oxytocin, a hormone we have as well. In humans, oxytocin levels are known to increase when we're feeling empathy and trust. The heightened stress levels brought the male rats together and their togetherness helped them cope with the stress. Pretty neat, huh? My experiences with male bonding were similar. My greatest connections with other men have almost always been through some sort of adversity or high-stress situation, whether it was the challenges we faced together at the boys home, the physical intensity of a martial arts class, a heightened imaginary circumstance in an acting class, or a drunken fight amongst friends that led to hugging it out afterward. There seems to be a specific pattern in males in group dynamics, particularly ones where there's a challenge, competition, or a threat, to come together and form strong bonds. I don't think I've ever experienced a stronger, more impactful bond in my life than these kinds of bonds.

In storytelling, these bonds are constantly highlighted: *Hamlet, Shawshank Redemption, Stand by Me, The Green Mile, Heat, The Deer Hunter, Lethal Weapon, Boyz n the Hood, Breaking Bad,* and more... but why? Why do so many men identify and relate with these kinds of bonds? Why do so many men connect this way and sometimes even intentionally put themselves in stressful or dangerous situations for the sake of forming these connections? One reason could be a need to express love to our brother. Men often show love to other men through acts of honor, loyalty, and even sacrifice such as having a buddy's back in a fight, giving a close friend a place to stay when he's been kicked out, or offering financial support when he's lost his job. We seem to have no problem showing our love to the men we care about when the shit hits the fan. It's the period in between those troubling times that a lot of men struggle to communicate love and value for one another, reverting to headlocks, slapping each other on the back of the head or farting on each other as a way to say, *love ya, bro.*

Without the adversity, we, men, do not have too many opportunities to truly show how much we care. Well, of course we *do*, but many of us struggle to or feel we don't know how. I believe this is part of the reason why gangster life appeals to so many men and so many struggle to give it up. The bonds are unbreakable. I certainly have tried to recreate the bonds I developed in the boys home since I left 20+ years ago, but to no avail. It isn't easy to generate the feeling of being locked up with someone and having lost virtually everything, nor do I really want to, so how could I recreate the bond that comes from it? I have, however, been able to put myself in group environments where there has been some element of shared challenge or risk, and it has produced great bonds.

I recommend all men find a way to experience this kind of bond between men. Unique from the other reasons I mentioned earlier that men need other men, male bonding can bring out something special in you, and if you've never experienced it before, I urge you to explore it. I'm not saying you can't join an all-male cooking class, sewing class or yoga class. Do anything that puts you around other men and you'll have opportunities to form bonds through common interest. But it has been the scenarios that involve physical aggression, risk or challenge leading to a shared vulnerability dynamic that have produced the bonding-through-adversity experience that deeply impacted me as a man. It changed me and it may change you, too.

A DASH OF VIOLENCE

In addition to adversity and heightened stakes, men often have some need for physical aggression and competition. Some even believe that evolution has shaped men to be warriors. If this is true, then, without a war, a warrior has little purpose, and may be left with a primal instinct to be violent. Chew on the idea that males may have evolved into warriors as a result of a long history of facing threats. What would that mean? Well, if we consider that we face a lot less threats today than we did thousands of years ago, wouldn't it mean that we're kind of *smack* in the middle of an awkward pivot in evolution? A bunch of men living with a primitive need to be violent in a world of less threats and, therefore, less need for violence... then what? The most obvious issue would be the one of controlling violent behavior, but we'd also have the issue of some men living with a part of their nature dormant. That's the part I want you to really chew on - the possibility that a dormant need for healthy aggression could be hindering some of us from fully developing our masculinity or reaching our potential as a man. Yes. I *am* suggesting that violence may still be a part of masculinity... and that by channeling it in a healthy way and creating an environment for it to flourish, we might develop unique connections with other men and with our own masculinity and virility.

If you agree that there may be some validity to the case I am presenting, what are some ways we can meet these dormant needs without breaking the law or betraying our values? Is there a healthy way to be violent? I think that depends entirely on your perception. We see plenty of non-threatening violence in sports and martial arts. Yes, some sports appear to encourage violence in a way that seems dangerous and gratuitous. I won't argue that. I will say, however, that when a sport or art form allows for physical aggression in a structured way that simultaneously enforces self-discipline, it can produce a healthy, liberating experience that remains safe and controlled. There are plenty of ways to be physically aggressive that have elements of competition and simulated risk that do not even involve man-on-man violence or contact. Rock climbing, archery, scuba diving and even weight training all have elements of physical challenge, aggression, competition or risk without man-on-man violence. They can produce feelings of a warrior experience, satisfy a primal need, and develop an unexplored part of a man that may directly contribute to the crafting of his masculinity.

Whether it's an adrenaline high through an extreme sport, a man-against-nature scenario, or a simulated act of destroying, these can all be done in groups of men to varying degrees of dedication, and I believe they all can exercise an important part of your temperament. You can sky dive once a year, take a martial arts class twice a week, or move to Japan and commit the next twenty years of your life to mastering the art of the samurai sword. However it works for you and fits into your life, consider trying something. Living vicariously through violent films or video games, purging through various art forms and even talking to a confidant are all great ways to get out aggression, but I find physical simulations of a warrior experience in a group scenario with other men uniquely satisfying.

If you're cringing with discomfort as you read this, I get it, and in my opinion, it's all the more reason to try it. I hated sports and anything physically aggressive as a kid. It was because I was thin, frail, uncoordinated, and didn't think I'd be good at any of it. I was terrified of getting hurt, but mostly dreaded the self-imploding doom of humiliation when I would inevitably fail and the team would lose because of me. Oh, the pressures of middle school and high school... they were fucking brutal. I certainly don't want to put that same pressure on you. This is more of a supportive push to try something if you've never tried it before. We can live our lives in response to the traumas or fears we've faced and never do anything physically aggressive or competitive, finding solace through acceptance that it just wasn't meant to be, *or* we can lean into the discomfort to see what we discover, possibly leading us to some deeply meaningful connections through mutual admiration with other guys. It's up to you. Ask your gut. Ask your values.

COMPETITION VS COMPARISON

Men can be incredibly competitive. I am. Whether it's a fun rivalry between friends or striving to be at the top of the class or team, I'm almost always in competition as a way to be my best self. My father always told me *ya gotta be the best.* I don't know if he just wanted to motivate me or if it's because winning has always been a personal value of his, but it's ingrained in me now... now that I have confidence in my abilities, that is. As a kid, it just made me feel angry and insecure. I never tried to win as a kid; not because I didn't want to, but because I never believed I could. I wanted to compete and I wanted to win, but I had no confidence or self-worth, so instead I'd just compare myself to everyone around me who succeeded. I'd obsess over all the qualities they had that I didn't, oozing with jealousy, resentment and self-loathing. Ugh. I know the feeling so well, even writing about it brings it back into the pit of my gut. It's like a dull, nauseating emptiness. I won't lie, I've felt it as an adult, too. Being competitive makes us more prone to comparing ourselves to others. The line between them can easily get blurred, but the feelings and behaviors they produce in us are wildly different. It took me some time to see the difference.

Putting yourself in group scenarios with other men, whether the common interest is competitive in nature or not, will most likely lead to competition. Men, as I mentioned earlier, I believe are competitive to a fault and I want to prepare you for the good, the bad, and the ugly vibes that can arise in that kind of environment. It can generate an affectionate brotherhood among male friends, and it can also be detrimental to a relationship or team. In order to recognize the difference, we will need to unblur the lines between competition and comparison, but also between healthy and unhealthy competition. It will hopefully help you have a more positive experience.

Competition *can* be healthy. You and your buddy decide to do a 30-day detox and compete with each other to see who can avoid the most junk food. Not only can that be fun, but it will likely produce better results than if you hadn't competed. Same applies to competing with a close coworker to see who can hit the most sales in a week or challenging a friend to see who can get to the gym the most in a month. These are healthy, friendly competitions that can produce good feelings, endearment, and positive actions. The same applies to groups of men working toward a common goal. If competing with one of your peers, whether he knows about it or not, inspires a positive feeling and motivates you to work harder to reach a similar goal, it could help the team. It could also turn you into an exemplar for other members of the group. Inspiration usually leads to positive actions and positive outcomes.

Another way that competition can be healthy is by getting you to value the journey and not just the outcome. Sometimes competitiveness shifts some of our attention from the end goal back to the learning and development of the process, which means more personal growth and a more enjoyable experience. This can actually bring the team closer and create stronger bonds among you and your peers.

Probably the most positive effect competition can have on a group is getting the members to reach their maximum potential. Sometimes, seeing someone else advance farther than you or overcome a hurdle you haven't can light a fire in you. It can push you to give everything you've got and use every tool in your shed. Healthy competition inspires action. It asks *what can I do to win fairly?*

Comparison is the thief of joy. Unlike healthy competition, comparing yourself to someone else takes all the joy out of the process and takes the focus off the goal. It obsesses over the person rather than the outcome. Comparison asks *what does he have that I don't?* It will extinguish your enthusiasm. Instead of feeling inspired and motivated, it stirs up feelings of jealousy and resentment. Comparing yourself to others compromises your self-worth and your objective and takes you off your path. Sometimes, it can even put you on someone else's path, causing you to lose your sense of self and behave in a way that betrays your character. Comparison takes all the value out of the process and goal, and your measure of achievement becomes entirely based on how well you can be someone else. It's a self-sabotaging setup for failure because you'll never be someone else as well as they can. Losing all focus on the goal sabotages the group, too, by dividing instead of tightening.

Recognize when it's unhealthy. Competition and comparison both involve sizing up someone else and seeing how you stack up. The major difference is competition involves actions that get you closer to the end goal, while comparison takes you off track. Oftentimes, comparison leads to inaction and self-destructive obsessing. It's personal. It's stagnant. Competition uses comparison only as a means to win and overcome the hurdles to the finish line. That said, even competition, while it tends to keep you focused on your goal, can still be unhealthy if you're not self-aware.

Here are a few ways to recognize when you're comparing or when the competition has become unhealthy:

1. You lose the value of personal development. You've become so focused on your goal that you stop caring about the process.

2. You lose the value of excellence. Your need to be the best is only for the sake of validation from others.

3. You lose the values of teamwork and honor. Your need to win has you diminishing or sabotaging your peers.

You can almost always rely on your emotions to tell you the difference between healthy competition and everything else. Healthy competition usually brings on feelings of inspiration, motivation, confidence, and excitement. If you catch yourself feeling any resentment, jealousy, insecurity or hatred, it ain't positive, big guy. Trust your feelings. Assess them whenever you find yourself sizing up another guy. Negative feelings can be regulated or neutralized by shifting how you frame your thoughts. Use your emotional awareness to recognize them before they have a chance to manifest.

Stay confident, focused, and supportive. The second I feel even the slightest bit of jealousy or any other negative emotion toward one of my peers, I take a step back and broaden my perspective. I assess the emotion, validate myself, and restrain my instinct to beat myself up for it. Then I generate confidence, focus, and support.

Confidence. For a boost to the ego, I go over my top strengths in my head and remind myself that I am skilled, talented, and unique and no one can implement my strengths exactly the same way I can. I think of my greatest achievements and remember the times I've been the most proud of myself.

Focus. I remind myself of my own journey. I'm not on the same journey as him. Even if we're on the same team and share a similar goal, our avenue there is unique and so is our personal process. I visualize my own path and return my focus there.

Support. Conscious efforts to be supportive of my peers has always resulted in positive feelings. Some of the guys I've felt the most threatened by have ended up becoming great friends. I start by saying something positive about the person I was sizing up even if I don't want to.

He's doing a great job and that's inspiring.
Man, he's really bringing his A-game. I can, too.
He's driven and ambitious. I value those qualities.

I'll even make an effort to give verbal praise to that person directly. A positive action that is the opposite of a negative feeling helps neutralize it and rebalances me.

Good job, bro.

These three things have helped me have a better experience in group scenarios with other men. Besides ensuring the vibes I contribute are positive, it also works as a way to counter any negative vibes coming from other peers. Rest assured, being great at anything in a group of men is going to spawn jealousy and resentment. You'll probably even have some haters. Learn to love them and stay confident, supportive, and focused.

Compete with yourself. If striving for healthy competition with others is too wobbly a path to navigate or too often produces a negative outcome, try competing with yourself instead. Every time you find yourself assessing someone else's strengths or achievements, turn the focus to your last greatest performance and use that as your benchmark instead. Each time you surpass your last best, your job becomes to outdo yourself the next time.

Lastly, every once in a while, remind yourself to value excellence over winning. Besides having a positive effect on your attitude, sometimes striving for excellence will result in a heavier focus on technique and lead to a better execution. Play around with what your driving force is in competitive atmospheres to learn what brings out the best in you.

EMULATING VS GENERATING

One of the reasons I think it's important for us to spend time around other men is to get inspired. When we see guys with characteristics that appeal to us, we will often - consciously or subconsciously - emulate those characteristics such as voice qualities, speech patterns, posture, mannerisms, and overall presence. Sometimes those characteristics eventually become a part of us. However, unless we're great actors or mimics, we could easily end up looking like a knock-off or fraud. It could hurt our character and make us come across as inauthentic, lacking identity, or trying too hard. I don't think emulation is exclusively bad, but those early stages of imposter syndrome that inevitably occur can be avoided. The next time you see a guy, in person or in the media, who displays a characteristic that you like, look a little deeper than the surface. What's the quality underneath the characteristic that's generating it? If he speaks in a deep voice, instead of trying to emulate *his* voice, ask yourself how he's generating that deep voice. Pay attention. Is it because he's centered and speaks from his diaphragm? Try generating *your* equivalent of the same characteristic by centering yourself and speaking from your diaphragm. If his walk and movements appeal to you, don't just copy him, try to find the *how*. In what quality is it rooted? What emotion, value, or strength is generating this behavior? Is it confidence? Zeal? Enthusiasm? Is it authoritativeness? See what happens if you try the quality on instead of the behavior, and see what it generates in your movement.

Generating is rooted in truth. It takes more work and the characteristic most likely won't be exactly the same as your model, but it'll be an authentic part of you. Practicing generating will help you understand the men you admire on a deeper level, and it'll eventually make the qualities you want to possess more accessible. Emulating is surface only with the hope that it'll eventually attach itself to some truth.

There may be some unique occasions when emulating will benefit you more than generating, for example, adapting to inside jokes, jargon, and other symbols that are part of a specific group identity or that bind a group together. This can be a little tricky. You'll probably want to feel like you're a part of the group but still be your most authentic self. Use your best judgment when trying to determine what is a key identifying symbol of the group you want to be a part of and be honest about whether or not you even like it. Be yourself. If you decide to emulate something, you might want to practice a bit at home before doing it in the group. Spend some time making it your own. Add your own spin to it to give it nuance so it feels authentic while still adapting. Adapting is accepting. Unfortunately, not adapting is often seen as rejecting and othering yourself. There is a sweet spot between maintaining your individuality and adapting to a group. Trust your instincts and always stay true to yourself.

HONOR VS ACCEPTANCE

Considering we no longer live in medieval times, honor is no longer really determined by the social group we're a part of. Sure, there're some exceptions, but, for the most part, this is now just referred to as reputation. Today, honor is mostly determined by you and your evaluation of your adherence to your own moral code, principles, and values. I'm noticing more and more that men nowadays rarely strive for honor for the sake of honor.

Instead, it's for the sake of acceptance. So many of the men I've worked with have expressed a need and craving for acceptance. Acceptance is a byproduct of honor. It's secondary. I believe a genuinely honorable man strives for honor as a measure of his worth to *himself* – as a man and as a member of the group to which he belongs. Of course, he loves the reward of acceptance. Of course, he loves the reward of praise and an admirable reputation. When those become the driving force, however, it just doesn't seem to have the same effect on a man's actions the way it did back in the Middle Ages. The self-consciousness and need for validation it produces today seems to crush a man's worth and hurt his development and moral compass. I see it taking men out of the moment and putting them in their heads. I see it creating gratuitous behavior. I even see it occasionally leading to false honor such as the exploitation of others, dishonesty, and deceit. Ultimately, I see it standing in the way of healthy alliances forming among male peers.

If you want other guys to flock to you and to want your friendship... if you want to be accepted... to be seen as a man of integrity... a righteous fella... a stand-up guy... then fucking *be* one. Based on the values, code of ethics, and common interests of the group you're a part of, figure out what a stand-up guy is to you. Then become that. What qualities would I respect most in a stand-up guy? Would he show up early every day? Would he stay late and try to find ways to be helpful? Would he be supportive and give praise to his peers whenever possible? Would he constantly set the best performance as his benchmark for success and work his ass off to surpass it? Would he stand up for himself? Would he stand up for others? Would he befriend the underdog? Would he be proactive? Would he organize meetings outside of the regular schedule for those who need help or want to work harder? Would he be courageous and take risks? Would he be willing to fail? Would he fall flat on his face in front of the group and get back up? Would he humbly accept criticism from his leader and peers? Would he participate in everything? Would he go first when no one else wants to? Would he never give up?

Honorable men are a dying breed because the world lacks noble exemplars from whom men can learn and get inspired. When men see true honor today, they value and respect it. They get inspired and they want it for themselves. I've seen it. It can foster some important and fulfilling ties between men. Be an exemplar in your group. Be the stand-up guy.

Bonding with other men can't be skipped. I believe it's a critical part of any man's journey to crafting his masculinity. Any artist who wants to become great consumes as much art as they can. It's how they feed themselves and get inspired. It's fuel. Seek out opportunities to bond with other guys through common interests, especially ones that have an element of simulated risk, aggression, or physical challenge.

Be mindful how much attention you give the success of your peers – it will keep your competitive feelings healthy.

Get inspired by the men around you by paying attention to the qualities they possess underneath the surface attributes you like, so that you can generate them yourself.

Always remember that being a man of honor does not have to be sought for the acceptance of others. Identifying what you see as honorable and then focusing on doing all the things that align with that will make you honorable to yourself. Revisit those values and principles you worked so hard on!

Spending time around other guys can help develop your social intelligence, nurture some primal instincts you may not have known you had, inspire you and provide you with opportunities to implement everything else you're working on to craft your masculinity. Find a tribe. Find several.

Learn to love men.

NOTES

NOTES

CRAFTING

MASCULINITY

Ch10: Optimizing Virility

(sexual appeal)

It should come as no surprise that when writing a book that helps men cultivate and craft the qualities they admire most in other men that there's a chapter on sex appeal. For our purposes, we're going to umbrella these qualities under the term *virility*. Virility and masculinity are both powerful words with layers of meaning and complexity. There are several sections in this book that blur the lines between virility and masculinity, but they're not exactly the same. Many definitions of virile refer to qualities such as vigor, vitality, energy and force, and often use the verb, *marked*, meaning shown or displayed. Virility can show through physicality, behaviors, anatomy, physiology and essence. The quality of virility is so innately identifiable to some that it's often defined as one quality even if made up of several. Masculinity, on the other hand, is almost always defined as several qualities or attributes that, together, create a characterization.

Virility comes from the word *vir,* meaning man, which specifically refers to the adult male; manhood or manliness. For the purpose of this chapter, it is most important to note that virility is associated with male sex drive or male sexual strength, though not specifically in regard to potency. Instead, it refers to the immediate association made between a man's marked physical attributes, behavior, anatomy, and physiology and his sexual strength. To put it simply, virility, to many, is the fundamental measure of the essence of a man's masculinity in direct relation to his sexual appeal.

After giving it much thought, reading a bunch of articles, and consulting friends trying to figure out what I should include in this chapter, I finally came up with what I think is a fun, albeit hodgepodge, collection of miscellaneous qualities you may find useful in crafting your masculinity that haven't already been discussed in the book. Some may enlighten you, some may seem obscure, and some may make you laugh. Take them with a grain of salt. We're delving deeper into the subjectivity and some of the inevitable essentialism and idealism of masculinity. None of these ideas are right or wrong. They're just ideas... real people's ideas - myself included - of what makes a man sexually appealing. Every man I know on a level deeper than the surface has either expressed or shown a desire to be sexually desired.

Body hair. In my reading and personal experience, I've come to learn that men with chest, arm, leg, and facial hair are more likely to be seen as having virility. One of the first signs of puberty in a male is sprouting hair in areas where hair has not been seen before. It distinguishes a boy from a man. Now, not all men grow hair the same. Some have very dense body hair, some straight, some curly, and some very little body hair or none at all, but have an impressive mane of hair on their head. Some can grow full beards and some sprout a little fuzz. You gotta work with what you got! Maybe think twice before your next man-scaping ritual. That hair that pokes out of the top of your shirt may actually make you more attractive to some. Perhaps, instead of getting it waxed, try just trimming it with clippers and a guard, or even letting it go wild.

As for facial hair, I like having a heavy scruff or intermediate beard. If you've always gone babyface, consider growing a light beard or mustache and seeing how it changes your face. Facial hair lets us cheat the contour of our face to appear more square, full, or thin. Talk to a barber or learn some tricks online. If you've always rocked a full lumberjack beard, consider going a little lighter and showing the shape of your jaw. Play around and see how it makes you feel.

Ironically, and I'm not just saying this because I'm bald, but less hair on the head seems to be more associated with virility than a full head of hair from what I've learned. Listen, I might give a finger or a toe to still be able to grow the thick, dark, curly Italian fro I had when I was younger, but I've come to believe that buzzed or bald is associated with higher testosterone and higher virility. Buzz it off?

Boldness. In regard to style, most of the men I consulted thought of blue denim, plaid, camouflage, and earthy colors when wanting to feel manly. I've learned that pairing those tones with something bold like solid black, white, or pops of red can highlight a man's virility. Curiously enough, the color red has been associated with power for centuries. Gotta love a good red tie.

Empathy. Yes, a man can obliterate his partner in the boxing ring and then later cry watching a puppy video. Both can be complimentary components of his virility and masculinity.

To most, empathy is associated with something positive and considered a desirable quality despite the contradicting messages many males may have been taught growing up. As I mentioned previously, virility is defined by signs of adulthood and maturity and, therefore, can be linked with emotional intelligence and even empathy. Sometimes, as a man ages and his testosterone decreases, his ability for empathy increases. In some cases, however, a man can have both high testosterone and high empathy. A double threat! The empathic man is deeply connected to his humanity, and seen as having both maturity and wisdom. For most men, empathy comes through conscious effort. Yes, life experience can increase it, but it's not promised. Developing your ability to identify and validate your own emotions is the first step in being able to recognize and understand emotions in others. Then you have to care. You have to take the focus off yourself, shut the fuck up and really listen. Be curious and really *want* to know what it's like to walk in their shoes. Don't stay at a safe distance. Get close and let yourself really feel what the other person is feeling.

Man scents. Funny one, but worth a mention since it came up a few times in my research for this chapter. We all give off a natural smell and we all have pheromones that affect the receiver. Our natural smell changes with age and is affected by several things, including what we eat. Get to know yours. The natural smell of a man is often associated with virility. Using scented soaps, aftershaves, deodorants, and colognes that compliment your natural smell can have an aphrodisiacal affect. You can also be daring and go all natural like I do.

Muscularity. It's the most obvious association with physical strength and physical capability. A moderate level of muscularity hits the sweet spot, indicating a man is self-disciplined and healthy but not self-obsessed or narcissistic. Muscle used to mean that a man does a great deal of manual labor or is an athlete. These days, we know it most likely means a man spends time at the gym. Either way, it's one of the biggest attributes associated with virility. It's also one of the biggest illusions of masculinity that many men like to hide behind. The easy access to steroids, which are often used as liquid virility and liquid confidence, only makes it worse. If you want muscles, I recommend you earn them on your own through hard work and diligence. Join a gym. Try a trainer.

Penetration. This is pretty cut and dry. A man's member is his most defining physical attribute. It should come as no surprise then that making use of it is connected with virility. Apparently, a man's relationship with his dick can have so much impact on his overall manliness that some folks have claimed his behavior is a direct reflection of how much pride he has in its size. Ha. I think maybe that's a bit of a stretch – no pun intended – excluding extreme cases, but I do think that utilizing your tool if you're able to is a great way to increase your own sense of virility. If you're not able to or have issues with potency, I think there are plenty of creative ways to be sexually intimate without penetration and still feel virile. There are some cases, however, when men are having sexual experiences where impotency is not an issue and they are intentionally avoiding penetration. I want to focus on that.

Guys who jerk off to porn excessively may want to consider closing the laptop and moderating how much they take in. I don't believe all porn is inherently bad for us, but too much can subconsciously create an unattainable standard that stops men from having healthy sexual experiences. When the person they meet doesn't meet the standard of their porn fantasies, a lot of men find themselves struggling to stay present, stay hard, or have an orgasm. They either end up fantasizing about their favorite porn clips or opt to just jerk off by themselves. If you've noticed this in yourself, it might be time to ease up on the internet wank sessions or even take a break for a while. I've had this discussion with several men and, after even just a week of abstinence, the vast majority have reported a notable improvement in sex drive and performance and more satisfying sexual encounters. Support is out there if you think it's an addiction.

Men who have sex with other men and insist on sexually being the recipient at all times may want to consider broadening the parameters. If you've picked up this book and you're open to doing everything you can to connect with your masculinity and virility, then consider swapping roles at least occasionally. If you've never done so before and you are absolutely terrified, it's all the more reason to boldly explore those uncharted waters. Nowadays, there are some fairly practical ways to get some practice by yourself before taking the leap with a partner.

Physical Self-Sufficiency. Different from muscularity, physical self-sufficiency is about being able to hold your own in the physical areas of life. That means everything from changing a tire to being familiar with a toolbox to defending yourself in a fight. As you may remember, the first time I sank a nail in one hit, I felt my masculinity/virility spike. I also see value in taking a martial arts class if you never have. Having the confidence of knowing you can protect yourself can affect the way you carry yourself and how you respond when faced with a threat. Criminals are usually really good at sizing up their targets. It's like they can take one look at you and just know whether or not you'll go down easy. It's not always about size and stature.

Zest. Charisma and a good sense of humor are manifestations of energy, vitality, and zest. Zestful men are positive, they smile a lot and simply enjoy things in life more than people who lack it. Zest happens to be rooted in courage. Yup, there's courage in living life with excitement, anticipation, and energy! To some, it's cheering shamelessly at a baseball game, singing loudly in the car, dancing like no one is watching, letting out a boisterous belly laugh, or even commanding the room with a well-timed, impressive fart to make your friends laugh. They all can be displays of zest. They all can say, "I live life with enthusiasm and, most of all, I'm fun."

The relationship between virility and masculinity is complex and at times can seem abstract and, like masculinity, the things that make up virility are, of course, not absolute or carved in stone. Nonetheless, understanding virility and optimizing your own can only support your craft of masculinity. Keep an open mind and if anything spoke to you that you want to try on for size, jot it down. You can find creative ways to turn some of them into realistic, achievable goals in the next chapter.

NOTES

NOTES

CRAFTING

MASCULINITY

Ch 11: Implementing It All

(self-sufficiency)

I knew I needed to discuss independence when I created the outline for this book, but I wasn't sure when and how. I started asking myself in what quality independence is rooted that is relevant to crafting your masculinity. I eventually came to *self-sufficiency*. It's the ability to hold your own as a man and survive in the world today, not just physically, but in all ways. It's different per individual, but things like having your own place to live, financial independence, and having a car if you live in a place where one is needed, are some common examples. Basically, it means you don't need to rely on anyone for anything. When I thought about what a chapter about self-sufficiency might look like, I wrinkled my face up. I didn't want to write about how to save your money and move out of your parent's basement. I needed to find another way to emphasize the importance of self-sufficiency and ways you can develop it, so I dug a little deeper. Besides the value of self-sufficiency, what do men have in common who are financially independent, proactive about their own success, and capable of handling life as it comes without leaning on others? They take action and they know how to crush their goals. They have honed the skill of strategically developing a plan and executing the shit out of it... and that's exactly what we're going to do in this chapter:

Implementation.

Living is doing. I believe the most self-sufficient men are doers. Show; don't tell. The best way we can earn respect is through our actions because anyone can talk a good game. Think about a piggy bank. It might make a whole lot of noise when shaken, but that usually means it has only a handful of coins in it. One that's packed full of coins and bills makes very little noise when shaken. People are no different. Those with a little bit of something tend to make more noise than what they can actually show for. People who have a lot of something often don't feel the need to boast about it.

Actions > Words. I know. I talk a lot about the importance of actions. They're everything to me. We are our actions. Now it's time to explore them in relation to goals and implementing them to achieve our goals. You've taken in a shit-ton of information in the previous chapters and now I'm going to show you how to translate all of it into goals and a well-structured plan of action. Let's go.

FORMULATE YOUR PLAN

The starting point for any solid plan is a crystal-clear objective or goal. A lot of guys know they're *supposed* to have goals, but don't invest the time or energy to choose them efficiently because they don't know how. They end up with a clumsy plan and then wonder why the towel gets thrown in after a couple weeks or months. Generic, rushed goals are rarely achieved. There's a process to setting smart goals for yourself. It takes reflection, strategizing, and time. When you put in the effort, you can formulate a plan that excites you because you'll know you can actually execute it. You'll be able to see a path and, oftentimes, a finish line.

Assess your life. Are you ready to put your entire life under the microscope? This is the time to call upon your ability to be objective so you can make an honest assessment of where you need the most improvement. Start by dividing your life into nine categories and ask yourself how satisfied you are in each area. Rate each area on a scale of 1-10. Once you've assessed each area, ask yourself "What do I want?" or "What will make this a 10?" Think about the parts of the book that you'd like to implement. In which areas of life do they need to be implemented most? Be patient and truthful with yourself. Write down or type your answers next to each area. There may be some crossover among the categories.

Career *(and education)*
Finances *(spending and security)*
Health *(and fitness, physical strength, body/voice)*
Social Life *(friends, peer groups, other men)*
Family *(parents, siblings and extended)*
Relationships *(marriage, dating, sex, virility)*
Spirituality *(religion, faith, nobility)*
Environment *(home and work space, town/city)*
Personal *(identity, self-development, emotional wellness)*

Get specific and real. *Make more money* is probably not going to get you anywhere. It's too general. You can make that more specific so that you'll know exactly what you're going after. *Double my salary.* Okay, better. It's more specific, but is it realistic? Do you believe you can actually achieve it? Let's make it more realistic. *Double my salary in the next five years.* Now we're talking. That probably feels attainable even if there's a big discrepancy between where you currently are and your destination, because you've given yourself five years. Goals that have a 5–10 year lifespan are long-term goals. Long-term goals usually have big discrepancies between the starting point and the destination. Having one or a few can motivate us to dream big, but too many can discourage us or stress us out. Pay attention to this when setting your goals. If you already have a few long-term goals with big discrepancies, assess how important they are to you. If you determine doubling your salary is less important to you than the other long-term goals you've already set, try turning it into a short-term goal, instead. *Get promoted to assistant director and earn a $5-10K raise this year.* Boom. That works and it's still specific and realistic. Short-term goals are goals we can achieve within about 3-12 months. There's no set number of long or short-term goals that are enough or too many. Start small and be conscientious about assuring they're realistic and specific.

Make them measurable. *Get a girlfriend this year.* Nah, buddy. Sorry. There's no way to measure your progress with a goal like that. It involves too many variables that are out of your control. You're going to have to reframe it into something you can break down into steps and actually measure. How the hell do you do that when what you really want is a girlfriend? Try focusing on the things you *do* have control over that will increase your chances of getting a girlfriend. Here are some examples:

- Be more proactive with your social life
- Revamp dating profiles with better, more recent pictures
- Face your fear of rejection and approach more girls
- Get into shape so you're presenting your best self

Each of these examples can be translated into specific, realistic and measurable goals. Getting into shape may translate to *Lose 20 pounds in 6 months* or *Gain 5-10 pounds of muscle this year.* Those are goals where your progress can easily be measured throughout the journey. Measurability of a goal is key for staying motivated and being able to problem solve or refine your plan if obstacles arise. Do this for all of your goals. Below are some examples of how crafting masculinity could look as a goal:

Identify my top four strengths and top four values, and memorize them in the next month.

Start a journal dedicated to risk taking and assertiveness, and document my progress in it every day for a month.

Develop a sitting and standing posture that I'm proud of and that resolves the tension in my back and shoulders.

Find a public speaking class that fits my schedule and register.

Practice up-regulating so that the feeling of confidence becomes so familiar I can self-generate it anytime.

Find a martial arts dojo near me that offers classes for men and start by next month.

IT'S EXECUTION TIME

Now that you've set specific, realistic, and measurable goals, you need a great execution strategy. Some of your goals will require daily habit-building and others will require weekly or monthly commitments. All of your goals will require some structure of action frequency. I like to create an actions list for that. Your actions list is your plan and constant reminder. It stays the same until you reassess your goals or feel the need to tweak an action to make it work better. It is not to be confused with your to-do list or calendar that is constantly changing. Some actions will need to be translated into to-do items, which we'll get into later. For now, let's build your actions list with four different categories: daily, weekly, monthly, and yearly. How you determine the frequency of actions for each goal is based on a few things.

How important or urgent is the goal? If your goal is to talk to your elderly grandparents more frequently, the frequency of your actions may be influenced by an understanding that they may not have a lot of time left. You may decide that daily or weekly phone calls are important. On the other hand, if your goal is to speak at a homeless shelter, the frequency of your actions may be influenced by how much this aligns with your values and purpose. If this is not necessarily your calling, but still something that gives you fulfillment, you may decide that once or twice a year feels right for you.

How much work is required to achieve the goal? If your goal is to lose 10 pounds in two months so you can have that six-pack in time for your beach vacation, you may decide that daily actions of clean eating and ab workouts are required to achieve that. On the other hand, if your goal is to blog more consistently to grow your business, you may decide that a weekly action of blog posting is sufficient.

How much can you afford to invest? This will likely be determined as you go through the first two questions. If your daily actions get too encumbered, you might need to reassess their level of importance and scale a few back to weekly. "Afford" in this case refers to time and energy investment. If your goal is to donate to a children's school, "afford" directly refers to your finances and you may decide that once a year is what you're currently able to invest.

Will your actions be repeating or sequential? Whether or not an action is repeating or sequential can help you determine under which category it falls. For example, if your goal is to pay off your student loans this year, monthly payments will probably make the most sense for you to achieve it. In this case, it's a repeated action and can go under monthly actions. A different example would be if your goal is to plan one trip this year. That will need to be broken down into sequential steps until your trip is booked. Think about what it will entail. You might need a few weeks to research destinations, request time off at work, book your flights and finalize your itinerary. In this case, I would categorize it as a yearly action, because it's a one-shot deal that requires a reasonably short-term execution plan. Occasionally, you'll have a goal that requires long-term sequential steps, such as writing a book. You'll likely go through stages of research, building an outline, character development, synopsis, and so on.

This is a long-term sequential process. You might categorize it under daily actions and frame it as *Invest two hours in my book.*

Build your actions lists based on your assessment of these four questions. Check out the sample. Note how every action starts with an action verb and ends with the goal it supports bolded and underlined. Action verbs get programmed into our brains, so make them as strong and specific as you can. Repetition of the goal will act as a constant reminder for why the action is important to you. You'll notice at the footer, I've included strengths and values. It's a little extra reinforcement that makes me feel good every time I see it.

ACTIONS

Daily

Read 1 hour to increase industry knowledge
Prepare clean meals for better ab definiton
Practice affirmations

Weekly

Write and share a short article to attract clients
Reach out every Sun & Thurs to talk to Dad
Lift heavy every MWF to build muscle
Organize & clean to keep a healthy living space

Monthly

Attend at least two social events to grow social network
Work two Saturdays to increase chance of promotion
Pay $500 to student loans until debt free

Yearly

Plan and rehearse two speeches
Plan one donation
Plan travel to two new countries

Bravery • Honesty • Kindness • Creativity

CONNECTION | GROWTH | INFLUENCE | EXPRESSION

ACCOUNTABILITY IS BOSS

I first heard it in the boys home. "Hold each other accountable," they used to tell us. Sure, it led to some gnarly fights, but it also led to us coming together as a team and facing our responsibilities. Accountability is a key player in success. It's all about ownership, responsibility, and commitment. Unlike responsibility alone, accountability can't be delegated. Accountability is about *you*. It's also the number one reason people hire coaches. Everyone can benefit from accountability. The most successful men in the world probably have accountability partners. Even a lot of coaches have them, myself included.

I recommend tackling your goals with a coach at some point, especially the goals that are connected to crafting your masculinity. Insight from someone who specializes in the areas you're focused on is going to have a major impact on your progress. While it would be great if you could have a confidence coach, speech coach, personal trainer, therapist, martial arts instructor, executive coach and more, you don't actually need a different coach for every chapter of this book. You can start with one. Try to find a life coach who specializes in working with men, and be sure it's someone who you can respect and might even want to emulate (or generate from). If you decide to navigate it on your own, here are some ways I keep myself and the guys I coach on track and accountable.

Integrate it. Your list of goals and list of actions work as a reference, and I recommend that you have a physical and electronic copy strategically placed where you'll see them daily for added reinforcement. You're still going to need to integrate them with your regimen and usual schedule. Add your daily actions to your to-do list or calendar for at least the first few weeks, until they become habits. Add your weekly and monthly actions and maybe set reminders for those. Those may stay on your to-do list or calendar permanently or until you've achieved your goal. The yearly actions will be translated over into daily or weekly steps when the time comes to plan them. Anything sequential needs to be translated over.

Be honest with yourself. You are your own boss of your goal progress. Be honest and fully objective in your assessments of that progress. Being too nice to an employee enables laziness, excuses, and doing the bare minimum. Being too punitive makes for an unmotivated employee who constantly braces himself for failure and, consequently, fails frequently. Being an honest and objective boss to yourself, and remaining positive, leads to accepting your own criticism and feeling motivated to make the necessary changes for a better outcome.

Recover from setbacks. Success is not measured by the number of times you fail; it's measured by how quickly and efficiently you recover from those failures. The road to success is hardly linear. You're going to fall flat on your face and step in a lot of shit along the way. Setting your expectations too high is a guaranteed setup for defeat. Be prepared for the setbacks and measure the risk factors of all your goals as best you can. Consciously practicing up-regulation and generating positive emotions can build an emergency reserve tank for the times you need it most.

Problem solve. When the shit hits the fan, those who hold themselves accountable take ownership of their own success and immediately begin seeking solutions. Those who don't hold themselves accountable sit back and watch everything crumble while counting all of the problems. The latter is a self-fulfilling prophecy of "I knew this wouldn't work." You have to fight that. There's no accountability in blame or helplessness. Change it to "I was prepared for this to happen, and I know I'll overcome it."

Then do your best to solve the problem, and use that emergency reserve tank if you need it.

Get feedback... wisely. Feedback and constructive criticism are essential for success. They help us gain perspective and improve. You'll likely be able to get feedback on some of your goals, but probably not all of them. Choose people who will be honest and unbiased, yet discern how much weight you give their feedback. It serves to widen your point of view only. It's not about praise or admiration. You do not crush your goals for validation from others. You crush your goals for you.

A SELF-VALIDATING MAN

Try asking yourself right now how much you need praise to stay motivated. It's nothing to be ashamed or embarrassed about, so be real with yourself. Keep the question in the forefront of your mind for a few days. Note how often you find yourself seeking validation from the people in your life. Pay attention to what you're feeling when you crave it the most or any precipitating circumstances that may have set off a need for it. This'll help you gauge when are the most important times for you to consciously practice self-validation. Let's say you discover the times you seek it most are in the workplace. The common feeling is inadequacy and the precipitating circumstance is a specific task that you never quite got the hang of. A seemingly logical solution might be to address the root of the problem by proactively investing time in becoming proficient at the task that makes you feel inadequate. That makes sense, but it could take some time and you might be in need of a more immediate solution. Try to neutralize the feeling with some affirmations. Hey, don't knock affirmations and mantras. They're another form of up-regulation and your idols and role models are probably all using them. Positive self-talk is a key player in validating yourself, but you have to do it in a way that's tailored to you specifically. General affirmations won't do shit. Here's what I mean:

"When I breathe, I inhale confidence and exhale self-doubt into the universe."

Does that do anything for you? If it does, great. Use it. It doesn't do anything for me. That's not the way I speak, so I wouldn't believe myself if I said it. I need to make it more specific and more *me*.

"I fucking *got* this. I'm a great employee and I'm getting better each week! I'm proud of my work."

That get's me excited. It makes me smile and makes me feel something when I say it. Do the same when creating your own affirmations. Use language that resonates with you. Keep it specific to the circumstance and always keep it positive. Negative words usually don't work. Avoid words like *No, Don't, Quit* or *Stop*. You can replace *Don't doubt yourself* with an equal and opposite positive action like *Trust your instincts* or *Believe in yourself.* The reason for this is if you have an instinct to doubt yourself, it's likely been programmed in your brain for years; instead of trying to tell yourself not to do it, try to neutralize it by doing the opposite. In this case, words like *Believe* or *Trust* could work.

Say your affirmations regularly. If you don't believe yourself, adjust the way you say them or adjust the wording. It has to prompt a positive response in you to work. Self-validation is an ongoing process we can practice as our need for it ebbs and flows. Our ability for it is rooted in our ability to creatively figure out how to give ourselves whatever it is we're looking for externally. The truth is, most of what we seek from others we can give ourselves.

SELF-SUFFICIENT... MOSTLY

Self-sufficiency goes beyond the ability to satisfy our basic life needs. It's also a measure of our emotional and intellectual independence. Emotionally and intellectually independent men usually demonstrate stability, a clear head, and an ability to self-regulate when under pressure. Where it gets a little hairy is determining how much self-sufficiency is enough and how much is too much. Taking self-sufficiency to the extreme can alienate you from others. It can even lead to narcissistic behavior or neglecting your other values. Self-sufficiency doesn't have to be so black and white; seeing it on a spectrum might help you stay aligned with the other values of yours.

Pre-navigation-app era, women loved to laugh at the guy who'd stubbornly spend an extra hour finding his way because he refused to pull over and ask for directions in fear he'd lose self-sufficiency points. I mean, I'm laughing, too, especially if the guy values time and efficiency. Striving for absolute intellectual self-sufficiency caused him to throw his other values out the fucking window. I believe we can do better than that. If we see self-sufficiency on a spectrum, we will be able to see that utilizing our resources is still mostly self-sufficient *and* aligned with our other values.

The same goes for emotional self-sufficiency. We all have emotional needs. Denying ourselves of them in an effort to achieve absolute self-sufficiency is a denial of our own humanity.

Remain objective and approach self-sufficiency with wisdom and a wide perspective to discern where your choices and behaviors fall on the spectrum.

CONCRETIZING GREATNESS

The virtue of mastery, as it's described today in connection with masculinity, is usually more in line with basic self-sufficiency, as in you need to be able to hold your own and not depend on others to get through life. We've discussed how it's an important virtue and component of masculinity, but there is more to life than simply surviving, and, in the context of crafting masculinity, choosing to go further can deepen your feelings of worth as a man. We live in a world where men are measured by what they can do for you. A man's capability to efficiently create, build, fix, solve, serve, teach, or lead make up a big part of his worth to the world. Knowing your strengths and values leads you to purposeful work, which is a key to your self-worth. Your worth to the world is another story. All acts of purposeful work do add up and make a difference, but when viewing yourself as an important piece of the puzzle that makes up mankind, could you distill your overall contribution to it down to one sentence?

I am a master of _________?

I learned to love photography in the boys home. They taught us how to make our own cameras using tissue boxes. I ran around with this ridiculous cardboard contraption, pestering staff and residents to let me photograph them with it. It was fun and I was good at it.

Later, in community college, I majored in graphic design and was able to take a bunch of photography courses. I learned about real cameras and spent hours in the darkroom developing photos, burning and dodging, using filters, and creating cool effects to produce the perfect picture. I fell in love with photography even more. I hoped I'd be doing the same when I transferred schools to finish my undergrad, but photography was not a major part of the new design program. In fact, there were no requirements for it at all. I was bummed. Fortunately, in most of my classes, students were given the liberty to design using whatever medium they wanted, so, of course, I used my photography whenever I could.

One day, as my teacher was critiquing a design I'd brought to class, he asked me where I'd found one of the photos in it. I proudly told him that I had taken it myself. Without any acknowledgement or skipping a beat, he named a few photo resources I could use whenever I need a photo for a design – because we're designers and we don't need to do that kind of stuff. At least, that was his position. Of course, I responded by expressing my love for photography and letting him know I had spent a few years diligently working at it.

"You're a designer, not a photographer." He replied abruptly. Huh...wha...how dare he? He doesn't know what the fuck I can and can't do.

"Actually, I'm both," I rebutted.

He looked up at me and gave me a shrug, submitting to my stubbornness. "Jack of all trades; master of none."

Those fucking words have echoed in my head since the day he uttered them to me. For years, I was determined to prove that notion false and, dammit, I could not. This life is short. We do not have all the time we want. We cannot do all the things we want, and we certainly cannot be masters of them all. Man, I would be a master writer, visual artist, photographer, actor, third-degree black belt in Taekwondo, celebrity life coach, psychologist, and more. How many freaking lives would it take to achieve mastery in all those things? Sure, I can do a little bit of all of them and I do, but I ain't a master at all of them. Does that make me a *jack of all trades* after all…? When faced with the thought of what my overall contribution to humanity is, *jack of all trades* just didn't really cut it for me. It didn't make me feel a great sense of pride or worth as a man in the big picture of mankind. I wanted more because I know I'm capable of more.

I am a master of leadership.

That makes me feel something inside. It lights me up and makes me feel like a king… a benevolent one! It makes me feel like I have an important role and something valuable to contribute to the world. It doesn't mean I can't still play with a camera, practice martial arts, book an acting gig, or continue to do all the other things that make me feel fulfilled. It simply means I needed to choose one thing to master – leadership – then commit myself to practicing it until I've reached a level of excellence. And that's precisely what I did once I realized I couldn't prove my teacher wrong.

Honestly, you could probably get through life happily being pretty good or competent at a few things. I believe a *jack of all trades* can still craft his masculinity and live a fulfilling life. I have met plenty of happy and successful men who were not necessarily masters of their trade. I think competency and capability (self-sufficiency) is a critical part of the journey to feeling a sense of worth as a man. But mastery… mastery is an option for the men who want more.

Remember, show don't tell. Living is doing and actions almost always speak louder than words.

Assessing your own life in an objective way and choosing goals that are specific, realistic, and measurable are key components to formulating a solid plan.

Execution of that plan is all about the actions that follow, as well as their frequency and structure. A great plan and execution needs a strong team. It's ultimately Team You, which can be a one-man team or a multi-person team, as long as there is honesty, support, and accountability.

Remind yourself that the whole process is for you. Crush your goals so you can be the man you want to be and live the life you want to live. Praise and admiration are great, and you'll likely get plenty, but you can also learn to give yourself whatever it is you need throughout your journey and that's going to help you stay motivated, focused, and reasonably self-sufficient.

When you turn your *aha* moments from the previous chapters into structured actions you can start implementing, you'll begin seeing the difference in the way the world responds to you... when you're not even trying to elicit a response from it... and it's kinda fucking magical.

virtual hug

NOTES

NOTES

CRAFTING

MASCULINITY

Ch12: The Way of Leaders

The man you are: the man you want to be.

Did you close the gap? Tighten it? Perhaps the distance of the gap hasn't changed, but no longer seems unconquerable. I hope through reading and implementing what's in this book you discovered that no gap is insurmountable. I hope you learned something about yourself you didn't know was there - a strength, a value, a purpose, a presence, a voice, a component of your masculinity or your humanity. If not, I think this would make a really cool coffee table book.

Now that you've finished reading it, I've got a question for you: What is masculinity to *you*?

Do the men you felt admiration and envy toward truly possess what masculinity is to you or is it something else entirely? Is it just an approximation? Do you view them any differently now? Perhaps some of them you'll hold in higher regard. Others may be demystified and lose their heroism. There is no perfect method to defining or crafting authentic masculinity. It's all in your head. Nothing has actually changed in the world since the time you first picked up this book and now; only you... and your perception. Don't minimize that, though. Perception is reality and yours can convince everyone around you that you're the epitome of masculinity.

I make a lot of men question their masculinity. It's not because I race cars, shoot guns, power lift, or fuck mad bitches. It's because I'm confident and comfortable in my own skin... and because I *love* my masculinity and embody the essence of that *exact* masculinity. I encourage you to do the same and to encourage others to do the same through exemplification.

Every man can learn to love himself and his masculinity through deep self-exploration and the right actions. Don't ever look down on anyone who hasn't learned the lessons you've learned or hasn't yet overcome the obstacles you have. Instead, use patience and understanding to show them how. Great exemplars don't divide; they unify. The people who don't get it yet are the most important people to reach. Shaming and judging them says, "I'm better than you, so stay over there." Compassion and understanding says "I understand you so let's come together. I want to show you, not tell you, how I became the man I wanted to be."

Not every man is a born exemplar, but any man can choose to become one, and the world desperately needs more men who empower other men with positivity. If this book changed your life or empowered you in any way, please share that empowerment through exemplification.

I didn't write this book to get rich. I wrote it because I want to make a few men happy and maybe save a few lives. I wrote it as a reminder to myself. I wrote it because it's one way of paying forward the wisdom and empowerment that changed my life. Keep it going. Live by example and you will guide others to success. It's the way of honorable men and it's the way of noble exemplars. It's the way of leaders.

LEO,

I get you now. You have the hardest job of any of the turtles. You face your fears every single day. You take on so much responsibility. And you probably feel more alone than any of your brothers. I understand that now. Aloneness isn't loneliness, though. There can be solace in aloneness. It's a choice. Besides, leaders are never truly alone. You need your brothers as much as they need you. You guide them, motivate them, bring them together, and help them overcome their fears and weaknesses. They give you purpose in return.

You're the one I feel closest to now. I turn to you when I need to get back on my path. I think of you when leadership gets hard or when I forget why I chose it... or when I'm just tired of being strong. You unblur my vision and put me right back on my path. Thanks, dude. No, really. I know I'm probably just talking to some inner version of myself, but... thanks.

Frank
May 2020, New York

artist unknown

ACKNOWLEDGEMENTS

I don't believe I would be alive, let alone writing this book, if it wasn't for my years in the boys home. So, my greatest debt is owed to the staff, teachers, and residents I developed close bonds with in the years I lived there. You guys helped me find my worth, my strengths, and my purpose, especially the bearded lumberjack and my amazing therapist, Dr. Tocco.

I'm grateful for the acceptance and support of the family and friends who have remained a driving force in all of my creative endeavors, no matter how bizarre. Some of you have even been heroes to me. Scott was the first to read the book in its earliest stages and help me give it form. My mother and Troy were victims to countless design concepts and called upon for brutal honesty. My friends, Tony and Ken, were accountability partners, helping me stay on track when life pulled me away from my work. Thyer and Anna were mentors, inspiring me, but also challenging me when I felt sure to probe even deeper. Tessa was the friend who gave me confidence that I could actually pull this off. Franco was the friend who gave me a platform to talk about the work. My buddies, Sean and Filippo, gave me positive reinforcement. My buddy, Rob, in LA, spent hours on the phone philosophizing with me about virility and farting. Thank you all for every conversation, every morsel of feedback, every word that contributed to my process.

I would have never had the knowledge and tools to write this book if it wasn't for the teachers, mentors and masters I had the honor to study under. Barbara Marchant gifted me with a deeper understanding of the power of actions and the wisdom, discipline, and specificity necessary to choose them. The years I spent in your class have been two of the most impactful years of my life. Charles Goslin taught me the beauty in disturbing people in a profound way and the parts of me I need to call upon to do it, while Bill Esper reminded me of the joy artists often deny themselves of acting before they think. Thank you both for your remarkably genius minds, and rest in peace to both of you. Page Clements helped me find my voice and Carol Reynolds helped me find my body. Pamela Scott helped me reconnect with my inner kid and Michael Pesce taught me to say *yes.* Francine Krimsky believed in me and has remained one of my biggest supporters and cheerleaders. I feel so lucky to have worked with all of you. Jack Donovan's book, The Way of Men, and our talks were a big inspiration for me to write this book.

Finally, I want to acknowledge my clients and everyone else who follows my work. You guys give me the greatest gift ever: purpose. Thank you for the space to express, challenge, create, share, solve, lead, and do the things that make me feel the most complete. This book would be nothing more than a handsome memento on my coffee table without you.

MORE ABOUT FRANK

After being incarcerated for the majority of his teens, Frank continued living in New Jersey with his mother until he finished his associates degree. He then spent 15 years living and working in New York City as an actor and life coach for men. He graduated with a BFA from Pratt Institute and went on to study acting and improvisation at William Esper Studio, T. Schreiber Studio, and Upright Citizens Brigade. He made several television and film appearances and was cast in live theater productions while he ran his coaching business in the Upper East Side area of Manhattan. He also previously worked as a graphic designer and bartender, studied Taekwondo for four years and has since taken up bodybuilding and boxing as a hobby. When he isn't obsessively peering deep into the darkest corners of the abyss of humanity, he loves traveling the world, horror movies, irreverent humor, spending time with his family, and his cat, Mooch.

This is Frank's first book, which he wrote during the COVID 19 pandemic. He has since moved back to New Jersey where he continues coaching men in person and virtually.

You can visit Frank online:
Website: FrankPaulVignola.com
Instagram: www.instagram.com/vignolagram

NOTES

NOTES

Made in the USA
Middletown, DE
30 August 2024